A History Of
THE OLYMPICS

May 12, 1982.
od Jenda a Zuzanka

Books by Xenophon Leon Messinesi

Meet the Ancient Greeks
Visiting Greece
A Guide to Greece

A History Of
THE OLYMPICS

DRAKE PUBLISHERS INC.

NEW YORK· LONDON

Published in 1976 by
Drake Publishers Inc.
801 Second Ave.
New York, N.Y. 10017

ISBN: 0-8473-1162-7
LC: 72-94857

Printed in The United States of America

CONTENTS

FOREWORD

The deep belief of the author in the Olympic ideals is reflected in this book, which should persuade the reader to become an adherent of the noble principles of the Olympic Movement. This book contributes greatly to the comprehension and dissemination of the Olympic philosophy and at the same time enriches the knowledge of the reader.

With the care of the widow of the author, Mrs. Ismene Messinesi, this excellent book has been published and we feel sincerely indebted to her.

OTTO SZYMICZEK
Dean of the International Olympic Academy

Athens 17 October 1972

PREFACE

A branch of wild olive, to crown the brow, was the prize received by the victors in the ancient Olympic Games, as the sole award, though, of course, there followed honor and glory immeasurable.

The Olympic Games were a religious festival. They were also an expression depicting a mode of life in which upbringing and education were of primary concern. The aim of the ancient Greeks was the upbringing of men, and women, to be as fully integrated as possible. That is to say they wished to educate the youth to grow up to be men harmoniously balanced in matters of culture, morals, intellect, character, and physique. Such men would be better citizens, to their own advantage and to that of their fellows.

The Baron Pierre de Courbertin, the renovator of the modern Olympic Games, was a reformer with a burning and unquenchable desire to improve understanding and amity among mankind. He was equally interested in serving the youth of the world as in contributing to the well-being of his young French compatriots. When Coubertin turned to the ancient Olympic Games with the purpose of reviving them, the Games as such were not his objective, but merely a means to an end, a medium upon which he could base and further his reforms.

The resulting Olympic Movement, from the revival of the Games, with which this book is concerned, is, according to Mr. Avery Brundage, President of the International Olympic Committee, probably *the greatest social force existing today.**

---

*Mr. Brundage is now Honorary President of the International Olympic Committee.

9

Coubertin started his campaign for reform and for the revival of the Games in Paris in 1892, having spent some previous short years in investigation. That which he set out to do, he did. It is, however, a different matter as to whether his objectives have been fully achieved. There are some who doubt it. This is due to the fact that world conditions and the tempo of life are far removed from the leisurely days of less than a hundred years ago, before the airplane, television, refrigerator and the rest. We can nonetheless assert with a very high degree of certitude that had it not been for the Olympic Movement and the resulting newfound love of sport, and competitive sport in particular, the world would have been more discordant and still more quarrelsome, less broad-minded and with less friendship and understanding.

To understand the Olympic Movement we should examine the history of the ancient days, the gradual emergence of similar ideals under a new cloak. We should investigate the present-day problems and trends, and perhaps we might then be able to look toward the future with greater hope.

A History Of
THE OLYMPICS

I
INTRODUCTION

The Olympic Games, which, as we know, occur every four years in different cities of the world are so-called because they are modeled on the ancient Games that took place in Olympia in Greece. How and why are they based on the ancient Games?

The Olympic Games of the modern era, which were revived in Athens in 1896, are not modeled so much on the form of the ancient Games but on the ideals that governed those ancient sports and athletics. It has been considered that this ancient ideology is one of the strongest influences on character formation. This may sound amazing, but in reality it is quite simple, as we shall see. Moreover, the stories of the ancient Games, and equally so the story of the revival and rapid development of the contemporary Games, are among the most fascinating that exist. The more we examine them the more absorbing they become.

The ancient Games, which continued for many centuries— over a thousand years in fact in their developed final form—were religious festivals held every four years, and as colorful as any institutions that have ever existed.

The story of the modern Olympic Games has quite another aspect. It is the story of a man who had a great ideal that guided him all his life and to which he devoted the whole of his fortune. This man, the Frenchman Pierre de Coubertin, believed that education in his country was very remiss. He considered that proper education for the young was ultimately one of the most important matters for the peaceful and good-neighborly development of the world.

The Baron Pierre de Coubertin was born on January 1, 1863, and died in 1937. As a young man he visited England and saw how games were played at Rugby school. Later, he visited ancient Olympia in Greece. He became firmly persuaded that what he had seen in England and the inspiration that he had received from the story of the ancient Olympic Games were matters for the deepest cogitation. These, he finally decided, should be combined and made into a basic plan for the future education of the whole world. He was not content to leave matters as merely fit for contemplation. Endowed with a vast knowledge of history and a magic pen, Coubertin started a campaign that was planned with almost military strategy and an incredible tenacity.

The story of Coubertin is one of the most romantic that exist. It is the story of a man who struggled against odds that seemed insurmountable, but it is the story of ultimate achievement.

We should, of course, inquire into these two different aspects of the Olympic Games separately, the ancient and the contemporary. What is it all about and why are they so closely connected? The ancient Games are, in a sense, the parents of the modern ones, and to understand the modern ones it is as well to examine the parents.

The Olympic Games were, as we have already indicated, more than anything else, a religious festival in honor of the gods. There were other games too, held in other lands of the Greeks, every four years, though in some cases every two. The games held at Delphi were in honor of the god Apollon, god of the arts, of order and of prophetic lore, as also the driver of the sun chariot that every day glided across the vault of the heavens from east to west. The games at Delphi were known as the Pythians, due to the fact that Apollon had slain the dragon Python. The games held at Isthmia, on the other, eastern side of the Isthmus of Corinth, took place every two years and were in honor of the god Poseidon, the horseman god and the god of the seas. In Olympia the Games were in honor of Zeus, the father of gods and men.

Thus the principles that constituted the guiding rule of the Olympic Games, since they were in the nature of a religious festival, were those of *justice*, which is of divine emanation. In the parlance of sport this is known as *fair play*. Not everyone, however, was allowed to take part in the Games. Each competitor had to prove that he was a man of honor, guilty of no misdemeanor, and he also had to take the oath that he would "play fair" in the competitions. The athlete took part for the honor of the city that he represented, but also as a thanksgiving to the gods, who had endowed him with such physical abilities and perseverance as might give him the hope and chance of becoming a victor. The competitors were not allowed to take their entries for the Games lightheartedly, just because they happened to be swift of foot, or strong or with powers of endurance and character to back their endeavors. They had to undergo compulsory training for ten months prior to the Games, the last month of which was in the proximity of Olympia itself under the supervision of the Games officials.

At the Games there were no silver cups, no medals, no money prizes. Those who took part were what we now call "amateurs." The word "amateur" comes from the French; it means someone who has a liking for something or other, such as sport. The athletes of old were not interested in breaking records and there was no timekeeping or measurements, no placings, only the winner. The amateurs of sport are those who go in for sport for sport's sake, those who play in games or participate in athletics because they have the spirit to want to do so for the fun of it. Games, sport, athletics to them are adventures—challenges that require endeavor of which satisfaction, the prize in fact, is that of achievement. When we speak of "success" or "achievement" in sports we should not mean winning or coming first, but having succeeded in giving the best performance of which we are capable. "The important thing is not to win but to be able to take part."

It was this element that Pierre de Coubertin realized as necessary in upbringing. He saw that education was not merely learning facts and figures, but building up character for later life, to be able to face odds and overcome them, to achieve and succeed, but always with such integrity and with the spirit of fair play that will give satisfaction, and that he also knew would bring happiness. Sport, he decided, was the one real and sure means of building up young people into sane, well-balanced grown-ups, not lopsided, but people who would be esteemed and get on in life.

We shall be concerned with many words whose meanings may be just a little vague, a fact that becomes clear when the attempt is made to translate them into another language. The words that will concern us are such as "sport," "play," "games," "athletics," "competition," "adventure." They all have something in common. They all challenge us to an endeavor in which we have to get the mastery, to succeed, to achieve. All these are events in which we participate from an early age, and in the case of "play" from the very earliest of ages. We have an interest in them for the rest of our lives. Our participation must be voluntary or else they lose their meaning for us.

We go to school to learn; the main thing that we should learn there is "how to think." Naturally we must also learn to know many things, after we have learned to read and write, though there are so many things that we have to learn out of school. The problems of life are getting more complicated, and games, contests, sport, adventure should also teach us how to think and to take the necessary responsibilities when facing these problems. Sport in all its branches should teach us how to act. In school we must do exercises and train to become efficient in each subject. By practicing sport and training for it we learn to face our difficulties and thus how to be able to act efficiently. It is a mistake to think that sport just gives practice to make our muscles stronger or to keep us bodily fit. Sport builds *character*. In the English language, when one acts as one should with the true nobility of human nature, it is said that such a person is a "sport," and in all languages they call a fine fellow a sportsman.

In the world today there are 128 countries with National Olympic Committees, each responsible for their country's participation in the Olympic Games, and also for the promotion of the Olympic Movement as well as the maintenance of the Olympic Ideals. At the head of the Olympic Movement is the International Olympic Committee, known as the I.O.C.

Let us then start by delving into the ancient Olympic Games, but not too deeply, without resurrecting too many legends, however picturesque, yet sufficiently to understand what it was that inspired Pierre de Coubertin and still is an unsurpassed inspiration to mankind.

II

THE ORGINS OF THE ANCIENT OLYMPICS

We have touched upon and given an inkling of the role that athletics and sport played in the upbringing of the ancient Greeks. The Olympic Games had, however, another aspect, equally important. They were conceived as an instrument of promoting peace among the turbulent city-states. The history of the development of the Olympic Games may not be so important to our purpose, but it is nonetheless well worth recounting in short, and will explain much.

The Games at Olympia existed from prehistoric times, though most of what we know about them is from legends, about which writers of the classical period in Greece have written, although even this was hundreds and hundreds of years after the origin of the Games. We now know that these legends, however fanciful they may seem to be in picturesque details, had a solid basis of truth.

Olympia of course did not invent competitive sports. Competitive sports were native to many countries. Hundreds of years before the Games started at Olympia as regular Olympiads, the inhabitants of Crete, the Minoans, had been very fond of sports, and the games there, like those at Olympia, had a religious flavor and significance. The Minoans were particularly fond of the exciting sport of bull grappling, or jumping over the bulls' backs in a spectacular fashion. We have mural paintings that have survived from before 1400 B.C. depicting these sports as also ladies of the court looking on. From vase decorations of the period, we can also gather that the Minoans were fond of wrestling matches and other sports.

The legends say that it was Heracles (called Hercules in Latin) who came from Crete and founded the Games at Olympia, and also that the god Zeus was born in a cave in Crete and came to Greece from there. On the other hand, famous archaeologists, such as Professor Spyros Marinatos, now tell us that the worship of Zeus probably originated in the lands around Olympia, whence the creed went to Crete, to return later to Olympia. The word *Olympia*, on the other hand, would seem to come from Mount Olympos in Thessaly in the northwest of the Greek mainland, which was considered the almost heavenly abode of the gods. The word *Olympia* would thus come from the worship there of the Olympian god.

According to the legend, Heracles came from Crete with his four brothers; at Olympia they had a race, which Heracles won. It was, according to the legend, this fact that since the race was between the five brothers, the Games should be held every fifth year, which by our reckoning means every four years.

At the time when Heracles is believed to have migrated to Olympia the land was inhabited by tribes that had descended from the north around 2000 B.C. and conquered the older inhabitants, with whom they later intermingled. These new conquerors were the Achaeans, who had gradually developed a high level of culture, that of the Mycenaean civilization. Then, however, about 1100 B.C. a new wave of conquerors, also from the north, descended along the Pindos range, the backbone of Greece. They were the far less civilized Dorians, who conquered by the spear and the sword, and brought with them arms of iron, which was a hitherto unknown metal in Greece. Civilization then took many steps backward and a dark period fell upon the land of the Greeks. Even the art of writing disappeared for several centuries. During this period the Games at Olympia, whatever their tentative form might have been, also disappeared.

The Dorians were halted for a time on the northern shores of the Gulf of Corinth; they made one of their centers at Delphi on the higher slopes of mighty Mount Parnassos, where the most famous oracle of antiquity later developed. It was perched high like an eagle's eyrie in wild, austere but majestic country permeated with a sense of awe. There the Dorians established an oracle dedicated to the god Apollon, a son of Zeus.

A certain legend, however, is almost contradictory, but can be taken in conjunction with the above. Apollon would apparently have sent priests from Crete to Delphi to establish his worship there. On arrival they protested that they would not be able to live in such a wild arid place, but Apollon assured them that they would prosper remarkably. The oracle that the priests established did indeed prosper and was respected by all Hellenic lands and beyond. Delegations were sent to consult it and it became very famous. Delphi was able to learn what was happening throughout the known world from its many suppliants and visitors and thus became also a sort of information center of the Hellenic world. The Greeks believed that whatever the soothsayers of Delphi (the *Phophytae*) pronounced was indeed the expression of the gods, whose wishes should be obeyed.

All the legends indicate, and are undoubtedly historically correct, that it was Delphi that played the major role in setting the stage for the Olympic Games that were to be enveloped with such ultimate fame and splendor. The men of Delphi, from whom the prophetic priests were chosen, were Dorians, as were the men of Sparta, their kith and kin. During the centuries that the Oracle at Delphi flourished the priests seem to have been ever ready to lean sympathetically toward the Spartans with a slight bias in their favor in their prophecies.

At the time of the establishment of the "Olympiads" in 884 B.C. the lands of the Greeks were only just beginning to settle down from the invasions of the Dorians, and culture was just beginning tentatively and timidly to sprout again, especially in the Peloponnese, which had the most deep-rooted traditions. The culture had not nonetheless reached the level of pre-Dorian days. The Spartans were still ambitious to conquer the city-states that they had not subjugated, and in fact it was not till a hundred years later that they overcame the men of neighboring Messenia, whose fertile valley had made them jealous for long decades.

Sparta was undoubtedly to blame, for it was warlike and its one thought was to be prepared for warfare, rather than to be content with the peaceful tilling of the soil. Perhaps the Spartans could not help themselves because they feared their vassals, who were ready to rise against them. The Spartans let their wives manage their estates so that they could be free to attend to their military training. They were thus always ready to pick quarrels, but Delphi wanted peace and prosperity in the Peloponnese.

There were two neighboring cities close to Olympia—Pisa and Elis. The men of Pisa were originally responsible for organizing the Games at Olympia, but the men of Elis contested this and claimed the right to this honor. The quarrel was settled in a treaty signed by the kings of these two cities and by the law-giving king of Dorian Sparta, Lycourgos. The legend connected with this says that Lycourgos was watching the Games when he heard a voice asking him why he—meaning the men of Sparta—did not take part in them. Lycourgos turned round and looked in the direction from which the voice had come; and seeing no one, he concluded that these had been divine instructions. So Ly courgos made a treaty with these two cities. The treaty was incised on a metal disc with the words written in a circular fashion and not in straight lines. A thousand years later Pausanias, who toured all Greek lands in the second century A.D. and described all that he had seen, says that the disc was still visible in the Temple of Hera in the Sacred Grove of Olympia, the Altis.

Elis is probably present-day Amalias, where excavations have been made in the last two years; it is at the southern end of the broad coastal plain, one of the most vast in the whole of Greek lands. The Spartans had never subjugated the men of the plain of Elis. Is it not likely that the Dorian brethren of Delphi had a finger in this treaty?

The provisions of this treaty gave the Games of Olympia their fame and splendor, for it was this treaty that established the Truce, which was called the "Ekeheiria." The word means the physical laying down of arms. This remarkable treaty made the whole region of Elis sacred, and no person bearing arms would be allowed to enter it, under the most severe of penalties, during the whole period of the Truce. Just previous to this there had been a year of very poor crops and concurrently a pestilential epidemic throughout the Pelopponese, whose cities in great perturbation had consulted the Oracle at Delphi. The Oracle insisted that the men of Elis should honor the Games as their forefathers had done, that is to say promoting once more the Games with religious reverence and splendor.

The Games soon became most famous and the institution of the Truce gave them an importance beyond compare. As the period of the Games approached the men of Elis would send Truce-Heralds to all the lands inhabited by the Greeks and proclaim the Truce and the Games. From the time that the proclamation had been received all warfare had to cease and those fighting had to lay down their arms. All who wished to go to Olympia, either to take part in the Games, or as onlookers, had to be given unmolested passage through the intermediate lands, both on the journey to Olympia and on their return journey.

After the establishment of the Truce in 884 B.C., Olympiads were held every four years. At first, from the records that we have, it would seem that the participants came only from parts of the Peloponnese, and the Games were thus more or less local, existing as a religious festival and foregathering of the tribes, for there was only one running race.

We are told that, during the sacrifices to Zeus by the organizers of the Games, a priest stood at the end of the stadium holding a torch. The athletes among the worshippers, that is the younger men, raced to the end of the stadium toward the priest. The priest handed the torch to the winner, who was proclaimed victor and had the privilege of lighting the fire at the altar for the sacrifices. The flame at the altar burned symbolically during the whole period of the Games, though of course at this stage it was not for long, for there was only one race and the Games lasted but a single day. It is this part of the ceremony which has been resurrected for the contemporary Games, when the Olympic Flame torch relay sets forth from ancient Olympia to the city where the Games are to be held. During the whole of the modern Games the flame from Olympia remains alight as a symbol of all those spiritual values that are innate in the Games.

Something of the sort probably took place for the next twenty-seven Olympiads, from 884 to 776 B.C. After this, that is including the Olympiad of 776 B.C., the name of the winner was given to the Olympiad. The first winner, in that Olympiad, was Koroibos (or Coroebus). The name of the city of the victor was also recorded, and it is from this that we can surmise that, at the beginning, only the surrounding cities attended. With the backing of the Truce, however, the Games gradually attracted competitors and visitors from the whole of the Peloponnese, and later from all lands inhabited by Greeks.

This date of 776 B.C., became the most important in the history of the ancient Greeks, though perhaps it would be more correct to say that this date became the most historical. The cities of Greece were separate states. Each had its own weights, measures, calendar, and laws. The year in each city was named after the archon of the year, or after the name of the person whom we might call the mayor. There was nonetheless a very close affinity among the cities, for they all had the same language, even if there were slight differences of dialect. They also had a common religion, although each city had its own patron goddess or god, who was equally acknowledged by the other cities, though not as the patron deity. It was quite impossible, however, for men of different cities to refer to any given time and know which year was meant unless they knew the list of the other city's archons. It thus became the custom for men of different cities to refer to the Olympiad named by the winner of the race, so as to indicate the year.

Later, although the names of the winners of the sprint race were retained, the Olympiads were given numbers; Olympiad Number One was that of 776 B.C. The year 772 was Olympiad Two, the year 768 Olympiad Three, and so forth. The year 767 B.C. would be Olympiad Three plus one year. The year 765 B.C. would be Olympiad Number Four minus one year. The year 776 B.C. thus became for the Greeks what the year A.D. 1 has become for the Western world today.

It was not till the 19th Olympiad, in the year 700 B.C., that we note the names of victors from beyond the Peloponnese and that the Games had become Panhellenic, which means of all Greece. It may be that the Panhellenic character was due to the fact that the Games gradually started to have more events than the single sprint race, or perhaps it was the other way around: that is, because victors started appearing from beyond the Peloponnese, the festivities came to permit of a larger scope for the Games, with more events.

How long did the Truce last? Many have argued about its duration and still argue about it. It does not really matter very much, for we are concerned with the ideology and the principles. At a given time before the Games, as we have said, the Truce-Heralds would set forth to proclaim the Truce. Mostly they would go by sea, which was the most rapid form of transport, and in Greece only a very few cities were at all distant from the sea. Otherwise the heralds would go by foot, for roads hardly existed and carts were used only for transport of goods, nor was horseback a common form of locomotion. One theory is that the Truce lasted for the lunar month covering the Games. This might have been ample in the early Games, but probably insufficient when the participants came from farther afield, including the Greek colonies of southern Italy.

The Games in their final form lasted five days and many visitors came earlier to pitch their tents and meet their friends and connections from distant lands. One lunar month would thus have allowed ten to twelve days to arrive and a similar amount to return home, which was possibly ample time for the early Games, for the Greeks covered an amazing distance by foot in one day. Another theory that has been supported, but that seems rather hard to acept, is that the Truce lasted ten months. This theory is based on the fact that the judges and those whom we might call the stewards of the Games were appointed in Elis ten months prior to them. The athletes too had to start training in their own cities ten months prior to the Games, and the last month they had to train in Elis itself, under the supervision of the Hellanodicae, the stewards or judges. During the period of the last month the stewards were responsible for seeing to it that there was fair play and that similar training conditions applied to all. The theory of ten months, whether based on this or on other arguments, is somewhat unlikely, as anyhow it would not allow for the period of the return journey home.

The Truce then was probably of a shorter period during the earlier Games, and may even have differed from city to city according to the distance from Olympia and the date of arrival of the Truce-Heralds. What concerns us is that the Truce was adhered to and that it corresponded to the religious significance of the Games. There were some very few infringements, remarkably few in fact and only in the very early days of the Games—remarkably few indeed when it is considered that the Games lasted for over a thousand years.

The Greek cities continued to quarrel and fight each other, yet every four years the Games brought them together, with the result that when danger threatened from non-Greek external enemies they were able to think of all that they had in common and together fight the foe.

We have already said that many other Greek cities held games somewhat similar to the Olympic Games. Of these the most important were the Pythian Games at Delphi in honor of Apollon. These Games lasted fifteen days; the prize was a laurel crown. The games at Isthmia in honor of the God Poseidon were held twice a year; the prize was a wreath of dried celery. In view of the fact that Isthmia was fairly close to Athens the attending crowd was very large, possibly even larger than at Olympia. The games at Nemea, not far southwest of Corinth, were in honor of Zeus and the prize was a wreath of oak.

The Panathenian Games were held in Athens every year, and every fourth year they were given special luster and significance and were then known as the Great Panathenia. They were in honor of the protecting goddess of the city, Athena. These games featured processions of torch-bearers, and in general there seems to have been more of a spectacular element than in the Olympic Games. Where the first Panathenian Games were held is not certain, but in later Hellenistic times, that is after the classical period, they were held in the Panathenian stadium, which in its reconstructed form was the site of the first Olympiad of the modern era, in 1896. It was only the Olympic Games, however, that were backed by the institution of the Truce, which was honored in all the lands of the Greeks, and it was no doubt this element that gave them their supreme importance.

The Games at Olympia maintained their high ideals even after Greece had passed the Athenian Golden Age of the fifth and fourth centuries B.C., when the greatest artists and thinkers flourished, though even then some elements of commercialism had already begun to appear and there were athletes who had an eye to the possible profits. The ideals of the Games nonetheless survived the Macedonian conquest by Alexander the Great toward the end of the fourth century B.C., but the Games deteriorated rapidly in idealism after the Roman conquest in 146 B.C., after the Games were no longer limited to Greeks but extended to Romans.

The religion of the Romans was fundamentally of Greek origin even though they gave their gods and goddesses different names. In the case of Zeus the Father they kept the same name, pronouncing Zeus Pater as "Jupiter." The Romans, however, did not have it in their makeup to appreciate the idealism or the spirit of the Games. Theirs was a more materialistic philosophy. The Romans wanted spectacular sights based on blood sports in which hundreds of gladiators and wild beasts, and later Christians, lost their lives. When the emperor, Nero, wanted to take part in the Games, he had not much regard for their nobility or the elements of fair play. He in fact took part in a chariot race, and though he gave only a comic performance and even fell from his chariot, he saw to it that his vanity was satisfied by having himself proclaimed the winner.

The Games continued until the three hundred and twentieth Olympiad in A.D. 393, after which the emperor Theodosios, who had become a Christian, issued an edict prohibiting them as being the worship of heathen and false gods and anti-Christian.

After this, earthquakes, floods from the Alpheus, and the incursions of the Goths under Alaric in A.D. 395 did much to lay Olympia in ruins.

For many centuries the spirit of Olympia slept, but it never died.

III
THE ANCIENT OLYMPIC GAMES

Ancient Olympia was never a city. No one lived there except the priests. The Sacred Grove, the Altis, was not large. It was somewhat rectangular and surrounded by a wall, its sides being only three or four hundred meters long. The Gymnasium and the Palaestra, the wrestling arena, were outside it, immediately to the west. Inside were the temples and the altars, the shrines and the other buildings. The two main temples were magnificent. The larger was dedicated to Zeus, father of gods and men, and the other to Hera, wife of Zeus and goddess of womanhood. The columns were of porous stone and not of marble, but they had superb marble pediments with statues, many of which still exist. The studio of Pheidias, the supreme sculptor of ancient Greece, was recently excavated, in ruins naturally, close to the palaestra. Here Pheidias spent some five years in producing the enormous ivory and gold-leaf statue of Zeus in his temple. It was said of it that either Pheidias must have ascended to heaven and executed the statue, or that Zeus must have come down to earth to pose for him. Unfortunately the statue was removed to Constantinople in the early Christian years and has been lost.

In the Altis there were also many "treasuries" erected by various cities. At one time it was also reckoned that in the Altis there were at least three thousand statues, for the most part of victors who had won three times at the Games.

Next to the Altis, to the east, was the stadium, which never had tiered seats, except for the judges, but grass or earthen slopes. The hippodrome, where the chariot races, were held was separate, much larger, and probably closer to the broad-flowing

Alpheus to the south. In the long history of the Games the sites of the stadion and of the hippodrome probably changed several times. To the west of the Altis and of the Gymnasium there flows a smaller river, the Cladeus, which nowadays in summer is but a trickle. Beyond the valley of the Alpheus there are high rolling verdant hills and in the distance mountains that seem to have a song of their own to sing on the skyline. On the north, sloping right down into the Altis is the egg-shaped Cronion Hill, so called after the father of Zeus. It is only a few hundred feet high, and on the top of this, according to ancient belief, the patron of the Games, Zeus himself, would come, invisible, and watch the Games. For several miles around Olympia there are smiling undulating hillocks. Further to the north is the large fertile plain of Elis, while to the west, but a very few miles, though hidden from Olympia, there glimmers the bluest of blue seas, the Ionian.

We may be permitted to interpose here one of those local myths so typical and so enchanting, which formed the very essence of the Greek poetical imagination. In their minds the ancient Greeks populated the glades and the glens with fanciful creatures, the nymphs of the hills (the oreids), of the bubbling brooks (the nereids), and of the oak trees (the dryads), as well as the fauns who disported themselves and played their reed pipes. The rivers were deified and personalities ascribed to them, and among them naturally was Alpheus, the god of the river. The gods had human characteristics, and most human amorous proclivities; thus we need not be surprised that when Alpheus fell for the beautiful nymph Arethusa, he decided that everything in war and love was fair, and that he would make her his own. Either the nymph Arethusa did not reciprocate, or thought that it was the privilege of any beautiful girl, or nymph, to have her beau not have all his own way, and that a girl should see to it that she was properly chased. So Arethusa, the myth says, wafted down to the sea, with Alpheus in hot pursuit. There she dived into the cool blue waters of the Ionian sea, and did not surface again until she had reached the distant opposite shores of Sicily. Gallant Alpheus dived after her and finally caught her up on the Sicilian shores. We are not told what they said, but we may presume that she thought that Alpheus had been slow in his pursuit.

The vale of Olympia is sunny, bright, cheerful, smiling. In ancient times there were more of the shimmering grey-green wild olive trees, the kotinos, which are still abundant. The hills are covered with the golden green pine trees. A gay note is imparted by the bright green of the vineyards, while the slender tall dark green cyperissus, pointing heavenward, counterbalance them in color, tone, and sobriety. The bright oleanders, like massive rose-bushes, glow white, pink or red, full of good cheer. Early in the year the valley is full of the light-blue diminutive alpine iris, while even from the beginning of January there is a profusion of many-hued anemones, followed later by the bright crimson ones that open out like daisies as if they had something they wanted to tell you. In spring too there are other flowers, roses, jasmine, wisteria and other flowering creepers. Later there are the wild huge mauve thistles and then the ostentatious sun-flowers.

In the summer it is warm, but the nights are always cool, though during the day the athletes of old felt that it was unpleasantly hot for the unrelenting struggle for supremacy in the events.

We should try to visualize Olympia during the Games as a grandiose festival and at the same time a vast popular fair with a mighty concourse of people. The athletes were in neighboring Elis and would arrive just before the Games. The lords of the Greek lands would pour in, some separately and some as part of the official delegations, known as the theories, from the various cities. Each delegation tried to vie with each other in pomp and splendor, except the delegation from Sparta, which was always sober in appearance and without any ostentation.

The crowd that foregathered was conscious of its common heritage and culture. Here they got to know what the other Greek cities were doing, how they were progressing culturally and materially, what was the fashion in men's wear, in sandals or the color of dyeing the beard. All were anxious to know what was new. All the poets would come and declaim their verses, while historians might read chapters from their latest erudite treatises, as did Herodotos and Thucydides, surely the greatest historians of all times.

There was something strange, however, about this vast concourse of people. Something that to us nowadays seems so curious, so incomprehensible. There were no women. Women, on the severe penalty of death, had to remain on the far side of the Alpheus, almost a mile away. Some say that this might have been a reaction to very early times, before the times of the Achaean descent, when life was regulated by a matriarchal system in which the women were the rulers. More probably it was thought that the presence of women was a distraction to the athletes. It must also be remembered that the men who took part in the events wore no clothes at all. The very word *gymnasium* is derived from *gymnos*, meaning nude.

It is said that the practice of running in the nude was due to one runner in one of the very early Olympiads whose belt slipped so that he lost the equivalent of his running shorts and, free from the encumbrance, won the race. Others later appreciated this advantage. Perhaps the slipping of the belt may not have been quite such an accident, and anyhow the Greeks had no prudery in gymnastics—that is, in exercising in the nude. It is worth noting that not all games were barred to women; indeed, at Corinth and at Sparta there were races for women only. It is not known whether the women also ran in the nude, for the Greek word describing their races stated that they divested themselves, but we do not know whether this meant of all their clothes. There are indications, especially from a statue, that they did not do so, but left one breast uncovered.

The Olympic Games were a great show, among the greatest that there have ever been. The athletes took part in friendly rivalry; the fact that they had all trained together in Elis for the previous month would have made the rivalry keener, and the friendship more pronounced.

The Events

The events of the Games were not precisely the same in each

Olympiad, nor necessarily the same in number, but the changes were very gradual, pretty much as is the case in the contemporary Olympic Games. An event may have been added after there had been several Olympiads without change. The total maximum number of different events was twenty-three, but owing to the changes there were never quite as many as this in any single Olympiad.

There were several of what we might call groups of events. There were some events only for youths, or what we might call the juniors. There were the chariot and equestrian events in the hippodrome and there were the combat events, though never with arms. The throwing and jumping events were never separate and only part of the pentathlon, or group of five contests.

There were various types of foot races. There was the stadium-length sprint, which until 724 B.C. was the only event; at that date the "diaulos" or double length sprint was added. The diaulos was not circular but from the starting line to the end of the stadium and back. The next Olympiad included the "dolichos," which has been stated to have been of twenty-four stadion lengths, or about three miles. Later still the "hoplite" race was added, in which the competitors wore armor but did not carry arms.

In 708 wrestling and the pentathlon, consisting of five contests, appeared for the first time. Boxing first appeared in 688 and chariot racing in 680, and then a single event with a four-horse chariot. At later Games a horse race was added, as was a short-lived race for a chariot of a rather cartlike type drawn by two mules, a four-colt chariot race and one for a two-colt chariot. Then there was the "kalpe," a race for mares in which the rider jumped down from his mare and ran the last part of the race, after what we would call coming into the stretch, and finished by holding on to the mare's mane.

The pankration, a sort of free-for-all catch-as-catch-can came in 648. It was the one somewhat harsh event in the Games, and it was held for boys in only one Olympiad, probably because it was considered too severe for them, though possibly because the programs were considered too overloaded.

The pentathlon was the most important event after the stadion-length sprint. We know the events but we are not sure in what order they were held, or whether they were always in the same order. We know, however, that the last event was the wrestling match, held by heats. In this event each contestant drew a number, of which there were two similar, so that the contestants paired off, the odd number being a bye. We should recollect here that there was no such thing in any of the events as getting a place, and that all that counted was who came first, the victor. We gather that if a contestant had already won the first three events, then the other two were no longer necessary.

The other events of the pentathlon did not count as separate events, and winning in them did not secure the award of a crown of wild olive branch. One of these events was a sprint race; another was the long jump. In this event the athletes held "halters" in their hands and by swinging them were helped to jump farther; in this way they achieved distances that, as recorded, amaze us today. The other two events of the pentathlon were the throwing events, of the javelin and the discus. There was also a pentathlon for boys.

The most exciting race was the four-horse chariot event. The bends were dangerous and the spills were frequent. The charioteers prayed to a special deity, Taraxippos, whose name means disturber of horses and who was believed to cause trouble to them. Winning required the greatest skill of the driver, as well as the best horses. Curiously, as in modern horse racing, the victor who received the crown of the wild olive branch was not the driver but the owner who had entered the chariot for the race.

The prize of the simple olive tree branch was cut with a gold-handled knife from a wild olive tree, the kotinos, close to the altar of Zeus, by a boy both of whose parents were living.

The Games at Olympia lasted five days. The first day was devoted to sacrifices and ceremonials, though it has been suggested that one of the two events not yet mentioned might have been held on the first day. These two events, which seem most unusual to us for inclusion in athletic games, were nonetheless included during the whole of the classical period. These were the contests for heralds and for trumpeters. We may of course remember that even today in the seaside resorts of Britain there are the town criers with their bells and calls of "Oyez, Oyez" and that they have an annual contest. In the Games the victor of these events was he whose trumpeting or voice carried farthest. The fifth day was also devoted to ceremonials and the honoring of the victors, while the other one of the events just mentioned, the contest of heralds or the trumpeters, was also held, as was the hoplites race.

The Pythian Games at Delphi, which lasted much longer than the Olympic Games, stressed the musical aspect, for the Muses came under the jurisdiction of Apollon. We should note that by "musical" was meant that which pertained to the Muses, or what we would call the fine arts, while that which we today call music, was then called mostly "harmonics."

The crowds saw to it that there should be fair play. They urged on their fellow citizens, cheering them to victory, but they hailed and applauded all the good performances of athletes from other cities. They yelled wildly and showered flowers and even fruit on the athletes they supported. The crowds spent the day watching the Games in the blazing summer sunshine and in some cases, such as that of the pentathlon remained until nightfall if the last event had not finished.

After the events of the day the onlookers would start enjoying themselves in a different manner, visiting tents of neighbors, friends or relations, discussing the events of the day and comparing them with the achievements of previous Games. Sometimes they banqueted at the expense of generous and munificent city delegations who might be celebrating the victory of one of their athletes. Cases have been recorded when the jubilant head of a city delegation, in his enthusiasm over the victory of an athlete from his own city, gave orders that the whole of the vast array of those present should be banqueted at his city's expense.

The crowds would gather around the competitors who had done well, proud to be seen in their company. Around them all, pretty well as in a fair today, there would be a throng of vendors of foodstuffs and drinks, of trinkets and of fabrics brought from afar. There would be the performers, the acrobats, and no doubt the fortune-tellers.

When the lucky and happy victor returned to his native city it was the tradition that instead of opening the city gates for him to enter, a small fraction of the city walls should be broken for him to pass through, for it was contended that with such athletes the city did not require walls to protect it. Further honors would await him. Statues might be erected in his honor while poets would laud him. Some of the finest poetry that has been written was about the athletes, especially that by the poet Pindar. It was also sometimes the case that an Olympic winner would be voted free meals at the city's expense for the rest of his life.

The athletes who entered for the Games would train at one of the gymnasia of their city; this was not merely a training and exercise ground, but in a sense also a sort of club and a scholastic center. There were also the palaestras, the wrestling arenas, which did not differ much, but which perhaps were not quite so esteemed.

At this stage, let us consider something regarding the life of the ancient Greeks and their upbringing.

To start with we should get them somewhat in perspective. To generalize about them might well produce an erroneous idea unless we include certain considerations. Instead of looking backward and investigating the past of some two and a half millennia ago, let us imagine the Greeks of ancient days looking forward to our epoch. Let us imagine them utilizing a telescope that they are trying to focus on us both in time and place. Suppose that they get this instrument wavering somewhere between, say, 1900 and 1970. Do not think merely of the material difference caused by modern inventions, but consider the outlook of the populations of the two periods. Think, for instance of the different status of women between these two dates. Think of the garments worn by women seabathing in 1900 and in 1970. Think of the notion of dancing in 1914 and in 1964.

So it is with the ancient Greeks. Their behavior in 600, 400, or 330 B.C. had in many aspects little in common. Think also of the same epoch in ancient Greece in, say, Athens, Thebes, Corinth, and Sparta. The ethics of the women had little in common in these cities, even at the same epoch. In the classical times the Athenians, for instance, adhered to the principle that excellence was to be found only in moderation and they practiced this principle in their meals. They ate most sparingly and rose from their meals still a little hungry, while the Thebans less than fifty miles away were positive gluttons. The Spartans, of course, were governed by the harsh communal dictates, while the Corinthians indulged in the advantages of mercantile wealth.

There were, however, certain aspects that were more or less universal, with the exception of Dorian lands, notably in the upbringing of children and youth. This statement holds good even for the Hellenistic times of Alexandria, two or three centuries after the classical age. It would be in many ways erroneous to say that the Greeks received a scholastic and cultural education and also a physical culture education. There was but one education, which embraced both aspects.

In the classical times in Athens, women were restricted in their freedom of action, though probably less than is often imagined. The restrictions imposed upon them were largely due to the utmost importance that the citizens ascribed to the upbringing under the mother's care and attention. A good and moral mother, the Athenians felt sure, was the prime requirement and essence of a well brought-up child. Let us also remember that the Athenians were members of the *demes*, or tribes, that the city life in the Agora largely took the place of home life, for the men, and that municipal life thus somewhat replaced family life. The boys had to be brought up, above all, to be good citizens.

The children therefore lived in the womens' quarters until the age of seven and the mother had the complete say and charge of their upbringing. Then the children were handed over to the tutors and to the coaches, the paedotribes. As the young boys grew older they frequented the gymnasia and the palaestras and there they not only practiced athletics and indulged in competitive sports but listened to the dissertations of the elders, the philosophers and the sophists.

One of the essential elements of education was the repetition and learning by heart of Homer, that is of the history of their forefathers, which was to them what the Old Testament was to the Hebrews. Homer crystallized the religion of the Greeks, and also taught tradition and ethics. Poetry, said Aristotle, was more important than history. Music and the rhapsodies of the bards were also prime scholastic elements.

Hippocrates, the Father of Medicine, elaborated the Hippocratic Oath, epitomizing the moral conduct of doctors, and it is valid more or less today. Later, when the cult of Asklepios (Aesculapius in Latin), the god of healing, became ascendant in the fourth century B.C., the all-importance of the contributive endeavor of the ailing person became the outstanding concern of the medicine-priests, who based their remedies on this. At Epidauros, which became the most prominent of the many shrines to the god of healing, the continued spiritual and corporal purifications formed the prerequisite to the cure. As well as physically, and perhaps more so, the patient had first to prepare himself spiritually and mentally.

At Epidauros was the immense theatre that then held seventeen thousand spectators, and in its restored form now holds fourteen thousand at summer performances of ancient dramas. At the theatre the tragedies were performed as a cultural elevation. At Epidauros also was the stadium where the non-ailing took part and the religious significance was not absent. The patients listened to suitable poetry and music and finally were prepared to visit the sanctum sanctorum, the room of "incubation" free of unworthy mundane matters, there in a trance to commune with the divine essence that lay in oneself, when the proper and harmonious physical, intellectual, spiritual and nervous tension tone had been achieved. It is interesting to note that this outlook in healing has still left its vestiges today since we think and say that those whose health "tone" is out of gear require a "tonic."

Such was the educational background of the boys and young men who entered for the Games of ancient Greece. In one of these palaestras of Athens was a wrestler who, we are told, was originally named Aristocles, although he is not known to us as such. This wrestler was sturdy and had broad shoulders, from which fact a nickname was given to him, the Greek word for broad being *platys*. His friends called him "Platon," and Platon, or Plato in his Latinized form, became one of the greatest philosophers ever known and, if we consider his disciple Aristotle a scientist rather than a philosopher, probably the greatest that the world has ever known. Platon not only laid the basis of the pre-Christian philosophy and creed, but was also one of the very greatest prose writers. Platon approved in principle of the education meted out to the Greeks, whereby the youth should be brought up to become fully integrated men. He, and some of his contemporaries, however, frowned on the overtraining of the athletes. They also did not like to see athletes with overdeveloped muscles, which was not aesthetic. The Greeks considered that that which was good was beautiful and that which was beautiful was good, and bulging muscles were neither. Moderation governed their lives. At the banquets, known as the symposia, intellectual conversation was as important as, if not more important than the food.

Warfare, unfortunately, plays havoc with education, and after warfare comes a period with debased ideals. The Truce of the Olympic Games was one of the world's greatest endeavors to ostracize warfare. Today, even if we do not confine ourselves to athletic meets, we have realized that conventions and congresses, from the United Nations to the professional international, foregatherings, foster understanding and smooth out incipient quarrels, as did the Games of old. Besides, the Games themselves taught mankind to be physically, spiritually, and culturally well balanced.

IV

THE YEARS
IN BETWEEN

The last of the ancient Olympic Games was held in A.D. 393. In the following year the edict of the emperor Theodosios prohibited the holding of the Games. Exactly fifteen centuries later, in 1893, Pierre de Coubertin urged the revival of the Olympic Games and on June 23, 1894, the International Olympic Committee, with Pierre de Coubertin as Secretary, and Demetrios Vikellas as President, was born.

What had happened in the meantime, in those fifteen centuries? What was the position of sport and what was the general attitude toward it?

It was just about the period that the ancient Olympic Games breathed their last and, not unconnected with the causes of the prohibition, that religious dogma, if not fanaticism, spread from Egypt and gradually affected the Christianity of both East (Constantinople) and West (Rome), in various degrees and for many centuries to come.

The new Christian religion was originally more Hebraic in character, but Basil the Great, who was born in Caesarea in Cappadocia in A.D. 330, completed his studies by visiting Athens and spending at least a few months attending the Academy of Platon, which still existed. As a result, through him, and with the assistance of the two Gregories, the Christian religion adopted an outlook more akin to the teachings of Pythagoras, Socrates, and Platon. Life after death was one of the principal implications of most men, whose main thought then became "how to save their souls?"

This new outlook, though based on the philosophy of their predecessors, was contrary to the outlook and practice of the ancient Greeks. In the classical days, these people, according to the Egyptians, "ever remained children." They loved their sports and games, and they loved the intellectual fun at the symposia. It was part of their nature and their culture. They trained their bodies for sports. The word for training or exercising in Greek is *askesis*. For the inhabitants of Egypt, who in the early Christian years were mostly Greeks or Israelites, this ascesis took on a new facet. They decided that it was against religious precept to practice ascesis to train the body, choosing rather to train the mind and ignore the body. For them, the body was only an unavoidable encumbrance of this transitory mundane life in the worldly passage of humanity on this planet, in the soul's journey toward the Kingdom of God.

Men started escaping toward the desert, the Thebaid of Egypt, to cast worldly life behind them, to become ascetes in its new meaning and practice asceticism. They started by going to the desert, living on the top of a column, or stele, as the steletes did, and then started forming groups to practice asceticism in the folds and monasteries. Even emperors laid down the scepter for the monastic hood.

This new doctrine taught that the desires of the body are sinful. There, in that city of Alexandria which had indulged in gastronomic orgies, the appetite for such things was now disdained. Monasticism also meant contempt for feminine charms, which were sins of the flesh, the turning away from marriage and from the bearing of children. The women, on the whole, behaved more as normal human beings, though some, neglected by the men, also betook themselves in pious devotion to nunneries.

This attitude, which was so contrary to the promotion of the notions of sport, lasted for several centuries, though in decreasing intensity. It also later inspired the Crusaders, who nonetheless, in the Holy Lands, in the Byzantine Empire, and the lands of Greece that they occupied and pillaged, behaved with anything but Christian integrity or humility.

The spirit of sport, however, could not be suppressed forever, and thus, centuries later, the institution of chivalry was grafted on to the code of Christian behavior. In this way, knighthood, though to a very limited extent, and only when it was expedient, became a revival of the Olympic spirit. The knights organized tournaments for jousting. Knights on horseback, facing each other replete with metal armor, would then charge in single combat with the objective of unseating the opponent by the thrust of the mighty jousting poles. Physical prowess, backed by courage, had come back into its own as competitive sport. The knights, moreover, pledged themselves for the honor of their fair ladies. The rules of jousting tournaments became as strict as those of the ancient Games, and fair play would appear to have been as sacrosanct as it had been in the years of yore. Sport was therefore tentatively to the fore again, though it was confined to a combat sport and existed only to a very limited extent, being practiced entirely for the aristocratic classes.

The common people were either not allowed or were not given the opportunity to participate in sports, and even if they might have been able to do so to some very slight extent, nobody was interested in writing about it. The youth, besides, only rarely received a university education. Even in Cluny in Paris and in the emerging universities of Oxford and Cambridge, the first in Europe, it was doubtful whether sport was possible at all. Youths who did not happen to be of the aristocratic classes passed to manhood either through the farms or through artisan apprenticeship, which hardly allowed opportunities for organized games.

There can be little doubt that there must have been more sport in the Middle Ages than that which has been recorded for us. The desire for sport is innate in all men, in varying degrees, in some races and periods more than in others. In popular festivals, in both undeveloped and peasant communities, it has often taken the form of dancing in which there are no organized judges, but where achievement is reckoned by the impression created on the opposite sex.

In Ireland from the most remote times great public games

were regularly held, as Dr. O. Misangyi has pointed out, but that country always had a tradition of community living and even a dislike for the institution of private property. It is said of the Irish today that when they see a street quarrel they wish to know whether it is a private fight or "can anyone join in?" In the highlands of Scotland there was a similar tradition of games, patriarchal in essence and based on the clans. These highland gatherings had something of the essence of the ancient Games, for they were not based on combat sports but on the physical prowess of the individuals.

Then in the eastern Mediterranean lands the rebirth, the "renaissance" of classical thought, was propelled by the advancing Ottomans from the lands of the Greeks, from Constantinople to Crete, and thence to Italy, to the West and the "Latins." Saving the soul was no longer the only thought, though it still held a strong hold and was important. The Renaissance brought with it creative art. Artists no longer confined themselves to religious subjects and ecclesiastical decoration. The myths of old were revived. Admiration of the beauty of the human body, which had been at the root of Greek art culture, intertwined with athletic expression, revived once more and showed itself in the masterpieces of the Italian painters. This rebirth also brought with it a revival of classical thought and genius, culminating with Leonardo da Vinci, the Aristotle of the post-Christian era, who even conceived of a flying machine.

With all this, nonetheless, the ideal of the fully integrated man, sound in mind and sound in body—a healthy mind in a healthy body—was neither appreciated nor yet understood. Yet somehow, a thousand years after the cessation of the ancient Olympic Games, chivalry in the first place and the Renaissance in the second had sown the seed and prepared the ground for the eventual revival of the ideals of the ancient Games.

Democracy, as the ancient Greeks knew it, and as we know it, was very late in sprouting timidly and unevenly in a very few cities of Europe. Possibly in Switzerland the idea of democracy appeared earlier than elsewhere in Europe. Sport requires the fertile soil of democracy to prosper, irrespective of the governmental form of the democracy, be it monarchical, republican, federal, or other. It is essential that for sport there should be a democratic spirit whereby on the playing field there should be equality among all. Even in the later middle ages, sport still remained the prerogative of the ruling classes and was confined to contests between individuals.

Gradually in the sixteenth century the idea of public games sprouted, here and there, like some timid flower of the fields. The power of the pen was beginning to be felt, for it was being backed by the power of the printing press. The Olympic Games of old were becoming known to a membership of erudite scholars. The Renaissance had fostered classical studies, and especially in the universities the story of the Olympic Games was becoming a subject worthy of the closest attention.

At the very beginning of the sixteenth century, in 1500, the French doctor Petrus Faber wrote the *Agonisticon,* describing the sports of the time. Toward the middle of that century the German poet Hans Sachs took up the theme, to be followed a decade later by the Italian doctor Mercurialis and toward the end of the same century by the Englishman Thomas Kyd. In the reign of James I, who ascended the throne of England in 1603, sport received royal support, and Robert Dover received permission to promote the Cotswold Games in Warwickshire as the "English Olympic Games," though they did not last long. These games were open to all, of all classes.

In 1608 James I founded a Golf Club, and this has its significance. In the modern era of sport there have been two developments that have been independent of the past. One was the formation of "sports clubs" somewhat resembling the ancient gymnasia. The other, which was a much later development and emanated from the clubs, as well as from the schools, was the innovation of team sports. Team sports have had the most profound influence on sport for all people. They constitute an institution the Greeks never knew. Team games also arose from the village greens in England, which was "common" land, held by all the villagers in common. There the "common" people held their fairs on the "commons," playing their games of cricket and bowls, and challenging the neighboring villagers.

It is certainly not our purpose to delve too deeply or unnecessarily into the history of sport and its rebirth. At the same time we should not ignore this period of its germination. Scientists, like businessmen, find it most profitable to look first at the past, then at the present, and then, either mentally, or by drawing a graph, to conjecture what will be the trend for the future and whether they are on the right path.

These stages of evolution have their own momentum, which accelerates with maturity. If we therefore have a look at the history of sport and are able to discern at approximately what stage we now find ourselves, we may be able to look into the future with more comprehension and perhaps with more trust and accuracy.

For many centuries after the period of its Greek blossoming sport was dormant, like plant life in the winter season. Then in the middle ages the delicate sport-plant surfaced from its roots under the earth. Perhaps nowadays we are still really in a stage of blossoming, and the prevalence of sport has a far greater future and importance than most of us are prepared to realize. It is interesting to note that the new emerging and struggling nations of the last two decades have given a thought to its organization that would have been inconceivable before the World War II. Let us then proceed with some examination of the development of sport.

Games may have been rare in the Middle Ages, but feasts and festivals were frequent, especially as the background of trade fairs. Group dancing was always a prominent feature and women were not more independent in many ways than they were at the turn of the present century. There were races and contests for women too. There is a race still held today in Thessaloniki of Macedonia, in which the women run while balancing baskets on their heads.

In England there was a big step forward when James I encouraged games in his "Book of Sports" for popular fairs, and even on Sundays. This liberal view was unfortunately soon followed by the restricted outlook of the Puritans, and once more retrogression set in. A similar situation prevailed in other countries.

The renaissance of sport did not really come until the nineteenth century, and really not until the middle of it. The renaissance of culture a few centuries earlier had paved the way in general but the soil was not yet really ready. The development of sport came in with the social and material change in the life of the populace, and so we might give this aspect a thought.

Little material progress was made in the world from the time of Julius Caesar and the Graeco-Roman civilization to the Napoleonic wars. The sea routes were sailed by similar vessels, the roads were of the same construction, and until the Industrial Revolution all methods of transport and communications remained relatively unchanged, except for one invention, by someone unknown, and passing virtually unnoticed, yet of the greatest importance—the horse collar. Apart from this there were in all these centuries two other outstanding inventions and one discovery. The one invention, for the good of mankind, was the printing press, and the other, for the destruction of mankind, and apparently first devised in China, was that of gunpowder. The discovery was that of the New World.

Toward the end of the eighteenth century two factors appeared that were to change radically the social outlook and the material conditions of the world, though as yet at a very slow pace indeed as compared with the second half of the twentieth century.

The first was the publication of Rousseau's *Social Contract,* followed by a wave of liberalism culminating in the French Revolution. The second was the birth of the Industrial Revolution in England at the same time as the publication of Rousseau's work.

V

THE NINETEENTH CENTURY

In the last three or four years the evolution of sport has taken on an accelerated momentum and the problems are therefore presenting themselves more acutely. The Olympic movement has on the one hand been making headway but it is being counterbalanced by the rapid changes of living conditions, habits, morals, and outlook. Not only have the unofficial and official outlooks on amateurism been undergoing the most rapid metamorphosis, but the intensity of this change differs considerably from country to country. There is a whole series of factors that is bound to make a very considerable change in sport, the outlook on it and the practice of it, within the next few years.

First of all there is not only the fact that the state, almost unnoticed, is intervening more and more in every aspect of our lives, but also the fact that the state is just awakening to the fundamental importance that sport should and will have in the future lives of all of us, but also to its responsibility in promoting it. The state is beginning to return to the ancient Greek notion that sport is inextricably bound up with education. Just as in ancient Greece the city-state provided the gymnasia and the palaestras, the state must nowadays provide the time for and the instruction for competitive and other sports, but it must also provide the places where these can be practiced. The state must so plan that the sport made available is basically voluntary, yet organized without being regimented. The state must now see to it that the architects and city planners make suitable provision for sports grounds and availabilities, for the schools, the civil servants, and the like. Most big industrial concerns in the advanced countries have already awakened to the fact of this need, as have many of the authoritarian states, but the state in the nations of the West is only just beginning to give anything like proper attention, because the national and civic authorities cannot do so without the backing of popular approval, and the public that counts and has its say and casts its votes in the committees and councils is not the public of the rising generation.

With the above thoughts in mind let us once more look back at the road along which we have advanced so that we may better appreciate where we are, where we are going, and where we *should* be going.

The soil on which contemporary sport was born was largely Britain and the lands to which the British migrated. It was not so much the character of the British that caused this, but rather those other circumstances that also resulted in the formation of the British outlook and character. The causes were many, geographical principally, which entailed causes historical and even more important climatic.

Britain, being an island, never suffered an invasion after A.D. 1066 and was able to prosper. It had to develop an administrative class to orchestrate its nineteenth century empire and to this purpose created the outdoor type in its schools. Its climate, far less cold than that of central Europe, has ideal playing fields in which games can be held in comfort throughout the year. The Industrial Revolution started in England largely due to geological reasons owing to close proximity of the iron mines and the coal fields, the two essentials of the times before transport had been developed. Sports were needed as a counterblast to factory life and even more so for those who worked in the mines below the surface.

Sport thus started in England with the advent of the Industrial Revolution, and probably not unconnected with it, and besides the seed had already been sown. At the beginning it was largely a matter of challenging contests, mainly walking, and this developed a sport that was then called "pedestrianism," which had an interesting background. The well-to-do kept in their service a man to carry their messages for friends or business connections. There was then no postal service, the postage stamp having first been used in 1840, and roads were bad. These men tried to perform the service now mostly covered by the telephone. Until quite recently the houses of the prosperous in England, as well as having a manservant called a butler, also had a "footman." The footmen, or pedestrians, were of course professionals, and their employers might back them in a contest against the employee of another, and even, not so infrequently, challenge them themselves. Pedestrianism became a heavy sport supported by heavy betting.

Two innovations unknown to ancient athletics first appeared on the British sports scene. One was that of timing and measuring athletic performances. The performances of the pedestrians were timed. Chronometers, according to Dr. O. Misangyi (formerly a chief chronometer at the Olympic Games), first appeared in England as early as 1731. The significance of timing and measuring in athletics is simply fantastic. These factors have changed the attitude of athletes. They race, jump, throw, and their opponents are no longer their fellow competitors but the chronometer and the decimal points of the centimeter on the measuring tape. Such measurement has given a tremendous impetus to athletics, but it must be observed that this is not necessarily a welcome outcome. There is a very great danger that it may be taking the element of sport out of sport. High performance is a laudable ambition, but it should not become the sole end.

The second innovation was the development of "team" sports. We have mentioned the evolution through the village green, but team sports found their fertile soil in the English "public schools," a name so misunderstood in the United States since these schools are not for the public at large but only for the sons of the well-to-do. Public-school games were not confined to games between the various "houses" within the schools, but flourished equally in challenges between the schools. The spirit whereby the pupils, or the students of the colleges assimilated themselves to their "alma mater" must have been one of the strongest formative forces in sports.

Xenophon Leon Messinesi (the Author).

Xenophon Leon Messinesi (the Author) in Olympia, 1968.

An ancient coin of Olympian Zeus to whom the Olympic Games were dedicated.

Early 5th Century B.C. statuette of runner from the museum at Olympia (inscription on the right thigh: "I belong to Zeus").

The Temple of Hera at Olympia.

The Palaestra at Olympia.

Race in armor.

Boxing.

Wrestling.

Four-horse chariot race.

The Acropolis—From the entrance to the Stadium decorated for the 1896 Games. Statue of G. Averoff in center.

Presentation of Prizes—The first Olympic Games at Athens 1896.

In the ancient Stadium of Olympia, the first torch bearer George Marselos, Greek champion, receiving the torch of the Olympic Flame from the Head Priestess (Aleca Katseli) for the Games of Tokyo, 1964.

The monument (stele) in the Coubertin Grove in the Academy at Olympia, which contains the heart of the Baron Pierre de Coubertin. In front West and East (winners of a cross-country race during the Session of the I.O.A. 1964) look on that which he would have liked to see.

In the Coubertin Grove, H.R.H. George W., LL.D., President of the International Olympic Academy, with lecturers. Left to right: Mr. W. Westerhoff, General Secretary of the I.O.C.; Jean Durry (France); The I.O.A. President; Prof. L. Diem (Germ.); Emil Zatopek (Czechosl.), long distance champion, Olympic Gold Medallist; Dr. Henry Pouret (France). 1966.

The Baron Pierre de Coubertin.

Mr. Avery Brundage, President of the I.O.C., and Otto Szymiczek, Technical Adviser of the Hellenic Olympic Academy, in the Museum of the Olympic Games at Ancient Olympia. (22nd February 1967)

The Dean of the Academy, Mr. Otto Szymiczek, surrounded by lecturers at the 1966 Session. On his right H.R.H. Prince George of Hanover, President of the I.O.A.; H.M. King Constantine of the Hellenes, Gold Medallist; Cleanthis Palaelogos, Deputy Dean of the I.O.A. On his left Xenophon Messinesi, Dean's Assistant and in charge of Public Relations (the Author).

Inaugural ceremony of the International Olympic Academy (1968) on the Hill of the Pnyx, Athens, Greece.

The ceremony of the Olympic Flame (1968) in the Altis, the Sacred Grove in Ancient Olympia.

The lighting of the Olympic Flame by the sun-rays with the help of a concave magnifying mirror, for the Olympic Games of Mexico (1968) (Head Priestess Maria Moscholiou).

The ceremony of the Olympic Flame. In the Sacred Altis with the Temple to Hera in the background, the Olympic Flame is lit by the light of the sun in a concave magnifying mirror (in center foreground).

Sides of two sepulchral steles. All eight sides have sporting subjects. 6th Century B.C.

Late black-figured lekythos. Circa 510-500 B.C. Introducing Heracles to Zeus.

Chris Papanikolaou, Greece. Pole Vault World Record Holder, 5.49m. 1969.

Lillian Board, British athlete in action, age 21. Lillian Board, who won European gold medals and an Olympic silver medal at the Mexico Olympics in women's 400m. event, ran her last race the 15th of June, 1970. The day before, she learned she was suffering from cancer.

Klaus Wolfermann, Germany. Javelin thrower. Gold Medallist in München, 1972, with new Olympic record—90.48m.

With the developing popularity of sport a new tendency became more pronounced—the distinction between the amateur and the professional. Sport had been the prerogative of the aristocracy but now it was equally practiced by the middle and lower classes. The prevalence of sport resulted in an enhanced interest in it, and this meant not merely participation in sport, but sport as a spectacle. The latter, with the resulting football leagues, football pools. baseball, basketball and the rest, has created armies of professionals, and has also created vast arrays of sport-fan maniacs. Coubertin had already realized the danger of this outcome and fulminated against the spirit created among those he designated as the "managers."

The distinction between amateurs and professionals in its strong antagonistic form arose from the old theory of fair play, for it demanded not only equal conditions for the competitors, but also equal conditions of training for them. The apprentice, the artisan, the laborer, whose livelihood required the exercise of physical strength, did not start on the same level, it was argued, as the young man who was being educated at a college. The college boy was to be brought up to become a harmoniously developed man, well balanced in mental ability and knowledge, in character and in health. The apprentice, it was thought, was not. He could not approach sport with the same mentality, it was fancied. Above all it was feared that the professional, whose livelihood depended on his success and achievements, could not be imbued with the same disinterested sense of fair play. It was particularly this latter aspect that was at the root of the matter, and still is, though with the aspect that class and education no longer have anything to do with it.

As for the women in the nineteenth century, they had not even been brought into the picture. The men did not want them that way, and the women of those times were ready to conform.

THE ADVENT OF THE SPORTS CLUBS

In 1814 the Pugilistic Club was founded in London with the participation of Lord Byron and other members of the aristocracy, but also with some good professionals. In 1816 the first gymnastic club was established in Hamburg, Germany. As early as 1817 a sports club was formed in England; it gave its members opportunities of training and competing. Other athletic competitions, as well as pedestrianism, were becoming popular, and one of the earliest was that of the long jump.

In 1859 came the first polo club in the Anglo-Indian army, and the first Rugby club, the "Old Blackheath Football Club." In 1863 we have the first athletic club, that of Mincing Lane, in the City of London, which came into being. These were purely amateur sports clubs.

Sport and athletics were certainly not the prerogatives of the British Isles, but it was there that they were principally developed into their present form, and moreover it was in Britain, in such places as the offices of *The Field*, a weekly periodical, that many of the regulations of the best-known sports were elaborated. Sport, as we have already said, also developed in all lands that the British colonized and where they had taken their ideas with them. This was particularly the case in the United States.

One hundred and fifty years ago the United States was comparatively thinly populated and as yet had not developed industrially. Yet there was all the open land in the world for all to enjoy sports, and the people pursued an open-air life, prospecting over vast expanses; thus the advent of sport was not long. In the United States it was in the universities rather than at the secondary schools that sports were first promoted. At first professionals played quite a prominent role, but by 1860 an "Amateur Athletic Club" had been formed in San Francisco. Even before this the athletes of the United States had already begun to shake the self-confidence of Britain by the high level of their performances, even if somewhat professional.

The humanist writers of the post-Renaissance period had had considerable influence in the revival of sport throughout Europe. Scandinavia and Germany promoted many sports meetings, mostly of their own flavor, while Switzerland was one of the first countries to indulge in them, although these countries did not have much subsequent influence on sports development in general. Spain had its own ideas in the passionately thrilling bull ring, which, however, does not meet with the general approval of the Western world.

In France? Well, in France the background was exactly the opposite of that in Britain. Britain did not have so much radically wrong in sports education and development that it needed a Coubertin to correct it, but France did, and that is why France produced him.

France was the country of the Encyclopedists, of creative thought and of artistic temperament. It produced a man who fitted into this picture, a patriotic Frenchman who wished not only to correct the evils of education that lay right before his nose, but, having spent his youth with the vivid pictures of international dissensions on his doorstep, as exemplified by the Franco-Prussian war of 1870, had an infinitely wider and longer vision for the world as a whole.

JUST BEFORE THE REVIVAL OF THE GAMES

Neither Pierre de Coubertin, the man himself, nor his work can easily be overestimated, yet they should not be wrongly estimated.

Coubertin's idea of reviving the Olympic Games was anything but entirely new, as we shall see, but it was his vision to realize that the ideals of the ancient Games could be oriented profitably in the .world in which he lived. The ancient Games, Coubertin realized, had united, at least for short periods at a time, the known civilized world of that epoch. The representatives of the city-states foregathered every four years under the aegis of a voluntarily guaranteed peace. They had the opportunity of getting to know each other better, of discussing matters of dissension between themselves, and as often as not, with a little goodwill, of smoothing them out and avoiding hostilities.

When Coubertin appeared on the scene the time-distances of the world had started to contract and narrow down, while the trumpetings of the newspapers had begun to bring knowledge of what was happening everywhere to everyone. Yet the coun-

tries of the world were still quarreling—as Coubertin, a Frenchman, knew only too well.

The Games of ancient Greece had been a great force toward
peace, backed by religious piety and ideology of nobility that
brought the Greeks closer to the gods, the gods whom they themselves had created. Protagoras, a contemporary of Socrates, said
that the measure of everything was Man, while Platon, a little
later, said the same thing when he declared that the measure of
everything was God.

Coubertin foresaw all this in the revival of the Games, and
found in them a measure that might lead to the creation of
equilibrated men, the fully integrated men who could be brought
together in the friendly rivalry of the arena, to understand and
appreciate each other the better.

The idea of the revival of the Olympic Games had already
been formulated earlier, in the seventeenth century in the Cots-
wolds and in 1779 in Worlitz in Germany, but there was as yet
no idea of revival correlated to the ancient ideology, but only
to physical fitness, except perhaps in Greece in the mid-nine-
teenth century. Elsewhere the revival was proposed mostly with
the notion of premilitary preparedness never entirely absent.

In 1790 the revolutionary Republican pedagogues of France,
Condorcet, Lekanal and Daunou, saw the possibility of a democratic leveling in the revival of the Games, certainly with the
idea of rounding up education for the formation of better citizens, but with a definite premilitary objective. Their idea was to
hold the "Olympic Games" in the Paris Champ de Mars—a name
appropriate for their misguided purpose. As Jusserand wrote in
Les Sports et Jeux d'Exercices dans l'Ancienne France (1901),
"To the military exercises were added under the Directoire,
which prided itself on its Hellenism, a number of public games,
revived from the Greeks, races, athletic wrestlings, chariot races,
held in the Champs de Mars. Voltaire without leaving his native
land could have thought himself transported to the Olympic
Games." Coubertin refers to the above in *The Olympic Games*
(1896).

From 1850 onward athletic games were being organized in

many countries of Europe and in the United States. The most note-worthy revival in the form of "Olympic Games," however, was in Greece itself.

In Paris, a Greek author translated the *Treaty on Gymnastics* of Philostratos, "for he had heard from the Greek students of that city," of whom there were many, that "the Greeks intended reviving the Olympic Games, and he thought that it would be useful to his compatriots for this purpose." The author, Minoide Mynas, published this book in Paris in August, 1858, with an addendum entitled "Regarding the Establishment of the Olympic Games in Greece."

The inspiration for the revival of the Olympic Games in Greece came from Evgenios Zappas, who was born in Epiros in northwestern Greece in 1800 and had fought heroically there in the Greek War of Independence of 1821-27. Later he migrated to Rumania and, assisted by his younger cousin, Constantine, acquired a large fortune. Like so many Greeks who have prospered outside their native land, he decided to devote his fortune to the benefit of his own country. He and his cousin therefore decided not to get married so that the whole of their fortune could be used for this purpose. Zappas donated a large portion for the construction of an imposing building close to the ancient Panathenian stadion and endowed it for the purpose of reviving the Olympic Games (the present-day Zappeion Building), which should include competitions of the fine arts, to be held in its halls. Thus the first Olympic Games of the modern era were promoted and held in Athens in 1859, thanks to the Zappas endowment.

The Games were repeated in 1870, 1875, and 1889, though they were to have been of a four-year cycle. They had varying degrees of success. Whereas they had next to no, or entirely no, effect on the success of the 1896 Athens Olympic I Games, it is interesting to note that the regulations elaborated for them, as also the program of events, were somewhat similar to those adopted thirty-seven years later for the modern Olympic Games, and must have had a paramount influence on the formulation of the first and subsequent Olympic Games.

Placings were not only for the victors, but also for the second and third places. The competitors had to give an oath (or promise) that they would play fair and not foul their opponents. The head of the state, King Othon, declared the Games open and distributed the prizes. The latter were announced ceremoniously, by a trumpeter and a herald, and included an olive branch crown for the first, an olive branch for the second, and a palm branch for the third.

John V. Crombach, in his *Olympic Cavalcade of Sports* (New York: Ballantine Books, Inc., 1956), mentions the first two of the Games but ignores the other two. He writes: "They failed essentially because the world was not quite ready and because Greece was not a powerful enough country or a rich enough country at the time to put over the idea." Greece was certainly poor, but the main trouble was that for the future Games the Rumanian government had sequestered the fortune made available by Zappas, as it did of all the Greeks who no longer lived in Greece. Crombach, however failed to point out that the Games were intended to be entirely Greek, for Greeks only, and for the promotion of Greek fitness, athletics, art, industry, and so forth. They lacked the deeper inspiration and vision of the international social force which was the purpose of the Baron Pierre de Coubertin.

The Games of 1859 already distinguished two categories of participants, the "Amateurs," called in Greek "Philathletes," and the "Professionals." These groups had to compete separately, but in essence the Games were entirely amateur; the professionals were confined to the equestrian sports, which were held for those whose business was connected with horses, that is dealers or drivers, with the idea of encouraging breeding. Apart from this, there were no professional athletes in Greece in 1859.

The 1859 Games were held not in the Panathenian stadium as originally planned but in the Ludowig (or Louis) Square, which proved inappropriate, and these Games were not successful. The 1870 Games were held in the Panathenian stadium, not yet reconstructed, but the crowd of thirty thousand was enormous for a city of then well under a hundred thousand. These events had a considerable measure of success. The Greek press, which had attacked the 1859 Games, lauded the later ones. In the 1875 Games the crowd, whose entry was free except for a few seats, behaved well, but the police control was ineffective. In these Games the entrants were exclusively from the University of Athens and were only several handfuls. Travel for the entrants was to be at their own expense but clothes and equipment could be provided for the needy by the Zappas endowment.

In the 1859 Games the events consisted of:

races: sprint, diaulos (double-stadion length), dolichos (seven lengths)
jumps: long jump, high jump, ascoliasmos (a hopping event)
throwing the discus: height, length
climbing the greasy pole
javelin: accuracy, length
equestrian sports

The 1870 Games added:

gymnastics
rowing (various events)
swimming (various)
chariots (carriages): with two or three horses and with two or three wheels
increased equestrian events (over the hedges)
tug of war
pole vault

The 1875 Games added rifle-range events, while in the 1889 Games weight lifting was added.

It will be seen that basically the Olympic Games events were gradually evolved. The two forms of the discus and the javelin were due to a misinterpretation of the ancient texts and were later corrected.

The ascoliasmos was soon discarded, as was the climbing of the greasy pole, which had its amusing side. Prizes were placed on the top, but the aspect that had not been considered was that the first participants gradually wore off the grease, making the climbing of the pole comparatively easy for those who were among the last competitors.

In 1888 Pierre de Coubertin wrote *L'Education en Angleterre*, but in the same year Philippe Daryl, also a Frenchman, wrote *La Renaissance Physique*, in which he wrote: "The Greeks, who knew everything or who foresaw that which they did not know, elevated and promoted physical culture, infinitely more than any of the modern states." After an inspired passage he continued: "Why should our professors and sages, ever bent on their texts, see only words and never the spirit? How have they not yet realized that the complete man is he who with the same hand wrote *Iphigeneia*, should also win the wreath at the Olympic Games?"

Full credit must be given to Philippe Daryl for seeing the educative and character-building values of the Games, but his vision was purely nationalistic. He thought of the Games before Coubertin, who, at that date at least, had not given any evidence of intentions regarding them. Daryl in fact wrote: *"Olympic Games.* It is a name that had to be said. We must also acquire our own. It is not sufficient for physical culture to be introduced, voluntarily or compulsorily into our schools; it must be taught sufficiently and take its due place in education as a whole, that is, the first place among all the lessons. . . . I visualize, every year in the spring, a great athletic contest in which representatives of French schools, after special competitive trials, will take part."

One of the most controversial sports subjects of this time was that of the status of amateurs and the prohibition of professional participation, but there was another. There was much debate on the English system of sports as opposed to the German idea of acrobatic gymnastics (the Pädagogische Grossmacht), which was contaminating the idea of sport in all the German-neighboring countries, including Switzerland, which seems to have been equally misguided. At this time football and tennis, with rules made in England (although tennis was French in origin), were spreading everywhere as ambassadors of English sport. French sociologists backed the English idea of sports, but largely to oppose the Teutonic idea of gymnastics bereft of the sports and play element and of the educative value. Numerous French educators, as well as Coubertin, visited Britain to study the British system on the spot. Many of them, however, while approving and admiring the sports of "perfide Albion," reacted against the idea of copying Britain. They found a compromise solution of opposing the Teutonic prototype and avoiding the British, in the idea of going back to the source, to ancient Greece, to the Olympic Games.

Coubertin arrived on the scene at the precise requisite time. The need of sport had acquired an accelerated urge in the minds of men. France, though not her educators, had realized the urgency of the need, and the world was getting ripe for it. *But* the world was chauvinistic, nationalistic, not ripe for the promotion of the amity of nations. Coubertin did not merely ride on the oncoming tide of sport, and graft the ancient ideology on to it; he did more, far more. He drove full tilt through the dissonance of squabbling nations, ignoring their petty egoistic jealousies and nationalistic prides, their ambitious politicians and rulers, and tried, successfully, to impose his remedy of "sport," for which his prescription was so simple: Revive the ancient Olympic Games but in a manner whereby the nations of the world would replace the city-states of ancient Greece.

From the time of Coubertin this budding world of sport has progressed at an incredible pace. It has probably not yet come to its first full bloom. Before passing away Pierre de Coubertin foresaw many of the dangers that could attack the budding flower and warned us against them.

We may be witnessing the first budding flower, just beginning to open out and admire it as one of the greatest humanitarian forces for the spreading of amity among nations. As Mr. Avery Brundage, President of the I.O.C., said in his address at the opening of the Fifth Session of the International Olympic Academy, on August 9, 1965, in reference to the XVIII Olympic

Games of 1964 in Tokyo: "No one who watched the parade of six to seven thousand participants from every quarter of the globe from nearly a hundred countries at the opening ceremony could have failed to be impressed. There were representatives of every race, every color, every religion, of capitalist, imperialist, fascist, communist, socialist and royalist countries, all following the same Olympic code of fair play and good sportsmanship. Nothing like this has ever happened in the world before." He prefaced this by saying: "The Olympic Movement today is perhaps the greatest social force in the world, now involving 118 [since then 128] different countries."

It makes one think. Where are we now? Where are we going?

We think that we see a broad vista ahead of us, a path upon which to develop freely without hindrance. This, of course, may or may not be so. So far the door for the future of sport has been opened timidly ajar. The nations of the world are certainly finding that they are becoming close neighbors. We are also realizing that sport, as Coubertin willed it, may be and is playing a major role in this new and closer relationship. At the same time we are aware that the state has more say in the direction of our lives, and that we are condoning it, very much as in the ancient Greek city-states.

VI
PIERRE de COUBERTIN

What immense satisfaction, you will say, Coubertin must have had in conceiving the modern Olympic Games, in establishing them and promoting them so successfully. Within his lifetime they became the chief interest and topic of the world during the fortnight in which they were held, and they embodied an idea that captivated the whole world during the intervening four years. Success, however, should not be measured merely by applause and fame, but by the extent to which the objective that you have set out to achieve has actually been obtained. Coubertin's success was phenomenal; at the end of his life, however, he could not have been entirely happy, for in the year before he died the Olympic Games were held in Berlin under the autocracy of Hitler, who wished to use them for the very purpose that Coubertin had been inspired to oppose and fight. The leitmotif of the Berlin Games was chauvinistic nationalism. The Berlin Games were a great show, the greatest so far, but they hardly furthered Coubertin's objectives.

Let us look at the main aspects of the life of Pierre de Coubertin: who he was, what his ambitions were, and also the ideals to which he devoted his whole life, and for which he fought with such ardor. We shall also consider the difficulties with which he was beset and how he outmaneuvered them. Let us, however, tell the story, just for the sake of telling the story, of describing an inspired fight of a great but comparatively unknown man. Whereas the results of his work are known, as he wished it, the man himself and his struggles have remained in the shade for most people.

As noted, Coubertin was born in Paris on January 1, 1863.

His father's name is given as Charles Louis, Fredy, Baron de Coubertin. The Fredy family originated in Italy, at Viterbo near Rome, where it had been well-to-do, but Pierre's ancestors were established in France by the fifteenth century, and at the court of Louis XI. A later ancestor of Pierre acquired the estate of Coubertin, close to Versailles, from which the family took its new name. The estate carried with it the title of barony, used by Pierre, but it would appear that they were never peers of the kingdom of France.

There can be no doubt that Pierre de Coubertin read *Tom Brown's Schooldays,* which appeared in a second French edition in 1874, when he was only eleven. It was probably the incident that most affected his life.

When he was twenty years old Coubertin decided to visit England, though apparently without any set program. He did, nonetheless, make a pilgrimage to Rugby School, where forty years earlier Dr. Thomas Arnold had been the headmaster and about whom one of the "old boys" had written *Tom Brown's Schooldays.*

The life led by the schoolboys as described in the book was the antithesis of the life led at the French lycées by Coubertin and his schoolfellows. The comparison fired the young Pierre and he determined to sponsor the English model, adapt it, and get it transported for the benefit of the young French schoolboys.

Coubertin sallied forth for this purpose with all the abilities given him by nature. These abilities were described by the late Professor Carl Diem, the staunchest standard-bearer of Coubertin's philosophy, in a speech at the International Olympic Academy in 1962: "He was a talented speaker and a fluent writer, a tireless and inspiring campaigner for a new education of the human race . . . at the same time a philosopher and teacher, historical researcher in gymnastics and in sport. . . . Above all he was a moral prophet, nay more, a pattern and a teacher of morality. He gave an example of self-sacrifice, even to the sacrifice of his fortune."

Coubertin was all this and much more. He was a psychologist, a tactician with the patience and the wisdom to advance toward his objective step by step, knowing exactly when to make a frontal attack and when to use the side door. He himself described his course of action as "to see far ahead, to be outspoken, to act firmly *(voir loin, parler franc, agir ferme)*.

Three years after his visit to England, in 1886, his articles on English education already showed that his ideas and his purpose had taken their direction, even if he had not yet conceived their final form and decided how he would achieve his aim. In 1887, when he was twenty-four, he wrote an article in *Le Français* that crystallized his ideas still further and made his compatriots sit up and take notice of him. He had cast the gauntlet. The essence of the article was that students had enough time to cultivate their bodies as well as their brains and should use their leisure hours for sports.

Coubertin followed up the onslaughts of his pen with practical activities when he formed the League of Physical Education. Within a year he had produced a plan for a "remedy by the offloading of work and reform of the lycées of Paris." He demanded the provision of three parks, or playing fields, around Paris and founded the Committee for School Sports.

By 1888 Coubertin was a full-fledged campaigner, surrounded by the equivalent of a general staff, all such men of distinction as Brouardel, the dean of the faculty of medicine, thus securing scientific approval and backing for his campaign. Also included were Jules Simon, former minister of state, and Fernand Lagrange, doctor and author. From 1889 Coubertin's pen was continually being dipped in ink, usually on matters regarding athletic education, the formation of societies, and the role of athletics.

Soon after this he became obsessed with the Olympic Games; this became an inspiring force that had to share the admiration which Rugby School had engendered. This was even before he had visited ancient Olympia in Greece. "Nothing in ancient history has made me ponder more than Olympia," he wrote, "this city of dreams, dedicated to a task strictly human and material in form." He first indicated his purpose of reviving the ancient Olympic Games in 1890 at a lecture in Birmingham, England.

It was not till some years later that he actually advanced to the attack. In his *Olympic Memoires* he wrote: "One evening in November 1892 . . . it was in the great amphitheater of the old Sorbonne . . . the reason was to celebrate a jubilee. Jubilee of what? The reason given was the celebration of the Union of Athletes. It was quite true that on the same date (November 25) five years earlier, two small Paris clubs had been invited and met to participate at a humble dinner for L'Union des Sociétés françaises de la Course à pied."

It was here that the proposal for the revival of the Games was first voiced. There was a historical lecture in three parts by three persons. Coubertin undertook the final part, concluding with the proposal "to investigate the reestablishment of the Olympic Games." He later wrote: "It was applauded. It was approved. I was wished a great success, but no one had understood. It was the beginning of a total lack of understanding. It was to last for a long time." This reaction was probably the best that could have happened to him. It showed him so clearly how gingerly he would have to tread.

He traveled to the United States and Britain in the next two years to test the reaction in those two countries, hoping that he would get more encouragement for the revival of the Games, but he was entirely disappointed.

Coubertin then decided to use what we would call a smoke screen, though he simply used the word "screen." In the French Sports Union and in the sports world generally a fierce controversy was raging on the question of amateur status. Coubertin availed himself of this, drew up a ten-point program for discussion at a congress, and included a variety of articles and subjects regarding amateur standing. They included such topics as "definition," "qualifications," "distinctions between sports," "betting" and the like.

Article 8, which found itself demurely inconspicuous, toward the end read: "On the possibility of reestablishing the Olympic Games. On what conditions could they be reestablished?"

After long and heated discusion on the earlier articles the eighth was approved, unnoticed by a weary audience. Next year two further articles were added: "Conditions to be imposed on competitors. What events should be included? Organization. At what intervals?" etc.

On June 23, 1894, in the great hall of the Sorbonne it was unanimously decided to revive the Games. Two commissions were appointed. One was to examine the amateur question, and the other, with the Greek D. Vikelas as president and Coubertin as secretary general, for the revival of the Games. The former commission got bogged down in eternal argument, but the latter was crowned with success.

Coubertin was at first in favor of holding the Games in Paris, but he was persuaded by the Greek delegate, Vikelas, to choose Athens. This suited Coubertin, for the second Games could then be held in Paris for the turn of the century when a great international exhibition was being planned for Paris. Coubertin finally became among the most enthusiastic for the choice of Athens and on this occasion said in his supporting speech: "The Greek heritage is so vast that all who have known physical exercise in any of its multiple aspects have been able to refer legitimately to Greece as its source."

It was not until after this that Coubertin decided to visit Olympia. He described this visit in his *Memoires:*

"One evening in November, 1894, I had just returned from Athens to France via Italy, having realized the results that had been obtained and the terrible fate that awaited me along the road that I had to follow. I remember ascending the winding path on the small hill on which the museum and the hotel were situated. A pure air redolent with pleasant scents wafted upwards coming from the banks of the Alpheus. The moon's light for a moment enlivened the vague landscape and the starlit night upon the two thousand years whose emotional contact I had come to make. The next morning I awaited the sunrise from my window and as soon as the first rays had spread over the valley I hastened, alone, toward the ruins. Their smallness resulting on the one hand from their close agglomeration (this lack of broad spaces so characteristic of the Greek and Roman civilization and so much in contrast to the Persian concepts) neither surprised nor disappointed me. It was a normal architecture from which I had to cull the teachings and this magnified all the dimensions. My meditation lasted all morning, alone and with only the sound of the bells of the herds on the road to Arcadia to disturb the silence."

The International Olympic Committe was formed with select, trusted, expert and aristocratic members who were to be, as they still are, not representatives of their countries to the I.O.C., but representatives of the I.O.C. to their countries.

The dates for the Games were settled, for the fifth to the fifteenth of April, 1896, (although in Greece the Old Style calendar was still in vogue and was then twelve days behind the New Style). The task before the responsible Greek authorities was enormous, to say the least, and far beyond the normal financial possibilities of the impoverished Greek government upon whom the burden must fall. Coubertin visited Athens and saw the Greek prime minister, Tricoupis, who told him as much but added, "See for yourself but it is not possible for Athens to hold the Games." Coubertin saw for himself. He called a meeting of leading Greek personalities, spoke to them at the Parnassos Hall, and decided that Athens was suitable. Many Greek patriots gave of their effective best.

The Zappas Olympic endowment helped but there were other factors that carried the day. A collection was started in Greece and special Olympic Games postage stamps were issued, the profit of which would be devoted to the Games. The Crown Prince Constantine, Duke of Sparta, and grandfather of the present Olympic Gold Medalist King Constantine, was full of enthusiasm and gave untold support, not merely by encouragement but by assuming the presidency of the organizing committee, which he conducted with the utmost energy and efficiency. George Averoff, a wealthy Greek, paid a large sum for the reconstruction of the Panathenian stadion out of gleaming white marble, on the site of the ancient one, retaining where possible some of the ancient tiered seats. It held sixty thousand spectators, but for the Games eighty thousand squeezed into it.

That was the beginning, but Coubertin did not rest. He was as energetic as ever. His pen never stopped. He wrote, with sports, internationalism and history as his main subjects. He also wrote on the political problems of Europe, colonialism, and similar subjects and continued to do so until his death.

In 1910 he wrote the article "The Spurious Sportsman," in which Callimatias, the hero, donned all the garb of fashionable sportsmen, talked their jargon, but was only interested in the effect he created. The book was full of humorous satire.

In 1919 Coubertin completed his four volumes of the *Universal History*. One can surmise that he had utilized the previous five years of World War I, when sport had almost been banished from the face of the earth, to devote himself to his other love, history.

In 1922 Coubertin left France finally to establish himself in Lausanne, Switzerland. No doubt he wished to back his international aims by living in neutral surroundings. And then, in 1925, aged only sixty two, he retired from the International Olympic Committee.

He gave his reasons: "I want to regain the liberty of my efforts to the service of popular teaching since I am persuaded that present society will not be able to resurrect itself from the accumulated ruins caused by its ambitions and its injustices and that new social forms will soon be imposed. I perceive in the prior dissemination of culture the sole guarantee of general progress."

Surely this act, supported by such a statement, proves conclusively that his revival of the Olympic Games was only a means to an end, a purely humanitarian and practical ideology.

There could be no finer epitaph for Pierre de Coubertin than one of his own last remarks: "In spite of certain disillusionments, I still believe in the pacific and moral virtues of sport. There are no political friends and foes on the field of sport, nor social, only men who are taking part in sport who remain in the presence of each other."

He died while taking a walk in the Parc des Eaux Vives in Geneva on September 2, 1937, aged seventy-four.

He was buried at Lausanne but he willed that his heart should rest eternally in Olympia. It was placed in a casket and inserted in a stele (monument) by the then Crown Prince of Greece, later King George II, and that stele now stands in the newly formed Coubertin Grove in the grounds of the International Olympic Academy, which is a memorial to the great Frenchman. It faces the ancient stadion, just across the road, though he had never seen it, for it was only brought to light in 1961. It nestles below the Cronion Hill where Zeus also watched the ancient Games.

The motto that Coubertin adopted for the Games was suggested by his friend Father Didon: *"Citius, Altius, Fortius"* ("Faster, Higher, Stronger").

For Coubertin the Games were the mirror of life. They were more—the introduction to and for him, the very essence of life itself.

Coubertin could hardly have left a greater legacy.

VII
THE MODERN OLYMPIC GAMES

The remarkable fact about the Games of the First (I) Olympiad held in Athens in 1896 was that the pattern set has required almost no change. Events, ceremonies, and the inclusion of women have been added, and also the series of winter sports. otherwise, the skeleton framework elaborated for the First Games has stood the test of time.

The Greeks themselves were so enthusiastic that they demanded that Athens should be the permanent home of the Games, as Olympia had been of old. This was understandable, for they had spent what for them was a huge sum of money, but Coubertin was adamant since internationalism was his major objective.

The participation was relatively small but the Games were a success, and they received world approbation. There were forty-two events in ten categories of sports, although the performances of the winners would not even bring qualification for participation today.

One of the features of the Games was the inclusion of the marathon race, for which a special prize was donated by an enthusiastic Frenchman and friend of Coubertin, Breal, a member of the Institut de France. The idea of the marathon race had not originally been included, but neither the offer of the prize, nor the appeal of the ancient Athenian could be overlooked.

According to Herodotos an Athenian hoplite runner (not Phidipides, as often stated, for he was the runner from Sparta) ran the forty-two kilometers (about twenty-six miles) from the

Marathon battlefield, in armor, after the victory over the Medes and Persians in 490 B.C., to tell the anxious Athenian citizens of the victory. If victory had gone to the Persians it would have meant the destruction of the city of Athens and the enslavement of the population. The runner, having reached the city gates, managed to exclaim, "Rejoice! We have won!" and then fell dead from sheer exhaustion. The story, though some have doubted its veracity, has always been alive in Athenian imagination, and the idea of the race appealed to the populace just as it had to the donor of the prize. It also caused much discussion, because many insisted that the distance was totally unreasonable.

The Marathon race was won by a Greek, Spyros Louys, and he entered the stadion to win among frenzied acclamation. He was carried on the shoulders of the younger princes to the king in the royal stand. Behind the story of his entry for the event there is so much that is picturesque that it is worth repeating. The training of Louys was most unorthodox, for he spent the eve of the race in chapel, praying, and on the day of the race he ate a whole chicken for strength.

The story of how Louys entered we give for what it is worth, but it has not been confirmed. It would appear that some days before the Marathon race the competitors would betake themselves to the village of Maroussi, some seven miles from Athens. Here there was a peasant who eked out a living by loading his donkey with barrels of water, which was good and plentiful in his village but rare and poor in quality in Athens. This peasant would lead his donkey with barrels of water to the capital, sell it for a modicum and then race back to Maroussi so that he could make a second journey within the day. Those who support the story give it as an example of the advantage of interval training. Louys for his everyday wear was dressed in the peasant costume of the white kilted *foustanella* and the *tsarouhia*, the gondola-shaped red shoes with colored pompoms at the ends.

The Games of the II Olympiad in 1900 were held in Paris, to coincide with the stupendous International Exhibition, which attracted all the public attention and completely diverted interest from the Games. The Games were anything but properly conceived or carried out and extended over many weeks. Coubertin was disgusted with them. The III Olympiad was held in St. Louis, Missouri, and the results were even more disappointing, for apart from another international exhibition that also stole the show, the European amateur athletes, who had to pay their own fare, found the venue too far and the journey too expensive.

Greece was in the meantime demanding that the Games be held in Athens again, and made a compromise suggestion that they be held every ten years in Athens, in addition to the normal Olympiads. Games were therefore organized for Athens in 1906. King Edward VII of England, whose queen was Alexandra, sister of King George I of Greece, visited Athens in the royal yacht *Victoria and Albert,* together with the British princes who later became George V, Edward VIII, and George VI. The Games were spectacular but, more important, they were carried out on the original lines, which have been followed subsequently. The I.O.C., however, did not finally recognize them as Olympic and baptized them an "Un-Olympiad."

The London Games of the IV Olympiad, in 1908, were the biggest success so far. Excellently organized, they received the enthusiastic support of the world press, although there were some Anglo-American dissensions.

The Games of the V Olympiad were held in Stockholm in 1912. Some nationalistic susceptibilities arose, but Coubertin tackled the difficulties with diplomacy and finesse and matters were ironed out.

The Games for the VI Olympiad had been alloted to Berlin, but because of World War I were not held. Here we should note that the Olympiad is reckoned for every four years, and, as in the case of the VI Olympiad no games were held, the next Olympiad, irrespective of Games, would be the VII (though actually the Games would be the sixth). Correctly speaking, therefore, one should speak of the Games of the so-and-so Olympiad and not the so-and-so Games. The VII Olympiad Games were held at Antwerp in 1920, but the Central European countries were not represented, not because they had been banned, but because the National Olympic Committees had not survived the ravages of the war, and it is these committees who are responsible for the representations that are ultimately sent to the Games, and incidentally give the final signature for the amateur standing of the entrants.

In 1924, at the request of Coubertin, the VIII Olympiad Games were held in Paris. The entries for the Paris Games were a record, numbering 3,092 (less than half the entrants for the Tokyo Games of 1964).

THE WINTER GAMES

The year 1924 has, however, another significance Skating contests had been held during the 1908 London Games, though not as official Olympic events. In the 1912 Stockholm Games the Norwegians (not the Swedes) would not allow winter sports, in order not to compete with their Nordic Games. The demand for inclusion of winter sports was nonetheless becoming more insistent and their inclusion was backed by Coubertin. There was a serious difficulty, however, in that the Winter Games could not be held at the same time of the year as the Olympic Games. Ice hockey had already been included after World War I at the 1920 Antwerp Games, and France decided to go further and add winter sports, which were held in the Olympiad year at Chamonix at the foot of Mont Blanc. In the following year the I.O.C. decided that there should be a separate four-year cycle of Winter Games and that the Chamonix Games should be recognized as the first Olympic Winter Games. Insofar as possible the Winter Games were to be held in the same country as the Olympic Games of the Olympiad and certainly in the same year. Since the Innsbruck Winter Games of 1964 the Hellenic Olympic Committee has also agreed that the Olympic Flame should be relayed from ancient Olympia to the Winter Games.

It should be noted that the I.O.C. makes the ultimate decision as to where the Games of the next Olympiad are to be held, and this is done a year or two before the previous Olympiad. It is never a question of allocating them to a country but to a city. Games were not, for instance, allocated to Belgium, but to Antwerp, not to the United States, but to St. Louis and Los Angeles, not to Japan but to Tokyo. When a city applies for the Games of a future Olympiad it must satisfy the I.O.C. that every appropriate arrangement will be made and even prove that the necessary funds, nowadays fantastically large ones, will be available. In the last few years some very well-known capital cities of the world have wished to have the honor allocated to them but their country's government has had to tell them that it could not afford it. The I.O.C. also takes many factors into consideration, and listens to the advice of the federations, but above all it wishes to see that there is a fair chronological allocation to the various continents, and that the various cultural aspects are included.

The IX Games were held in Amsterdam in 1928. The X Games were held in Los Angeles in 1932, where for the first time there was an important innovation, a significant one—the creation of an Olympic Village in which the contestants lived together. This was found to be most beneficial for the rapid promotion of a spirit of fraternity among the athletes. It was, in fact, a reversion to the ancient Olympic Games, where all the competitors lived together in neighboring Elis for one month previous to the Games.

The XI Games were held in Berlin. The entries exceeded four thousand for the first time, and here the ceremony of relaying the Olympic Flame from ancient Olympia, which was such a success, was first instituted. Torch runners brought the flame all the way from Olympia. It should be recorded, however, that a flame had been lit at the Amsterdam Games in 1928, though not originating in Olympia.

The XII and XIII Olympiads were bereft of Games, which were canceled owing to World War II. In 1948 the first postwar Games were held in London, for the second time, at the newly constructed Wembley stadium. In 1952 the host city for the XV Olympiad Games was Helsinki in Finland. In 1956 a new continent was chosen for the XVI Olympiad, and the Games were held in Melbourne in Australia. In 1960 the Games were carried magnificently in Rome, while in 1964 at least equally superb Games were held in Tokyo, Japan.

Such is the short historic catalogue of the Games of the modern era, prior to the 1968 XIX Olympiad in Mexico City, and the Games of the XX Olympiad for 1972, held in Munich, Germany.

In 1931 Coubertin stressed: "The Olympic Games are not international championships, but *festivals*, festivals of passionate endeavor, to spur on ambition, festivals of every form of the youthful urge to do great deeds." He in consequence attached the very highest importance to impressive if not reverent ceremony. The year before he died he said: "I therefore think that I was right in trying from the outset of the Olympic revival to rekindle a religious awareness." He gave his deepest thought to devising the ceremonials and in fact said that they should be devised "little by little, so that spectators and competitors might not be surprised by it." The Olympic Flag was not raised at the Games till 1920, and that was also the first Games at which the Olympic oath was given, though nowadays it has been changed to a "promise."

At the opening ceremonies of the Games the I.O.C. appears as host. The President of the I.O.C. conducts the head of state of the country in which the Games are being held to the seat of honor and presents him to the other members of the I.O.C. who are present.

The national anthem of the host country is then played and all the participants march past, with the Greek athletes at the head and those of the host country in the rear, with the athletes of the other countries in between in alphabetical order. Then they form up and face the Lodge of Honor. The president of the I.O.C. asks the head of state to declare the Games open. As he does so the Olympic Flag is raised, pigeons are released, guns boom and the Olympic Hymn, composed for the 1896 Games, is sung.

Then comes the great moment for which all have been tensely waiting. It has caught the imagination. Its course has been followed for many days, if not weeks, more especially in the host country but also by all the world. The last of the torch runners enters the stadium and runs right across it to light the flame that will burn till the end of the Games.

The first torch runner has taken the Olympic Flame from the hands of the Priestess lit by the light of the sun in the Sacred Altis in distant Olympia, by means of a concave magnifying reflector. The Priestess and her retinue come into the ancient stadion of Olympia, with the flame in a ceremonial crater (bowl), and it is here that the torch that is to be the first on its way is lit from the crater. The first runner then goes to the Coubertin Grove, close by, and lights a flame at the altar, before proceeding toward Athens. From Olympia it is carried by torch bearers, one for each kilometer, about 340 in all. In Athens it passes by the Panathenian Stadion, and thence to the port of the Piraeus, or to the areodrome. If the Games are to be held in Europe the torch speeds its way to its destination completely by runners overland. In the case of Tokyo, each torch bearer, from the southernmost point of Japan, was accompanied by at least ten runners, so that one hundred thousand runners, it is said, accompanied the Flame in its lengthy course to Tokyo through Japan.

Nothing of all the ceremonies seems to create such an impression as the Flame which comes from Olympia, sometimes as much as two months on its way. It links the Games about to be held with the religious expression sanctified over the centuries.

After the lighting of the Flame the "Oath" or rather nowadays the "Promise" is spoken. The parade of the athletes is then concluded and with it the opening ceremony terminates.

The closing ceremony is simpler and is performed by the President of the I.O.C. The Olympic Flag is lowered and there is a salute of five guns, presumably for the five continents and the five rings in the flag. Since Melbourne there has been no march past in the closing ceremony; now all the athletes enter the stadium, the idea being that they are now all of one Olympic family without any nationalistic rivalries.

The other ceremony to which Coubertin attached the most absolute importance was that connected with the prize-giving. He was insistent that it should be the personal endeavor of the athlete that should be honored, as it had been in the ancient days. That is why the stadium is emptied when the prizes are given. The three medalists should have the whole attention of the spectators. The winners stand on three steps, the central one being a little higher for the gold-medalist. The President of the I.O.C. takes the medals or insignia from a "maid of honor" and presents them. The flags of the winners are raised and the anthem of the gold-medalist's country is played. It was with the same spirit of honoring individual endeavor that Coubertin objected to the allocation of points for wins and placings, and no official ranking of participating nations is acknowledged, although this does not prevent the press from having its say, and computing their own points tables.

The International Olympic Committee

The first Committee formed for preparing the revival of the Olympic Games, in essence the first I.O.C., was nominated on the basis of a proposal by Coubertin. There were fourteen members from twelve countries. The members of the I.O.C. are the ambassadors of the I.O.C. to their native countries. Whereas the National Olympic Committees make their suggestions as to who should be elected members of the I.O.C., it is the latter that makes the decision, and not necessarily from among those recommended by the National Committees. It is essential that they should be independent and have no political implications. There is no fixed number. The I.O.C. prefers to limit the numbers of any given country to one, or at the most two, but there have been exceptions. The countries with two members are mostly those countries in which Olympic Games have been held. At the moment there are seventy members from fifty-four different countries. The members are elected for life and cannot be removed, but there has been a decision that those elected henceforth will be retired at the age of seventy-two. The President of the I.O.C. is elected by ballot by the members. Two vice-presidents are elected for an Olympiad period, and additionally there are five other members who together form an Excutive Committee. An I.O.C. Session is held every year, normally in autumn, and in the year of the Olympic Games there are two Sessions, the extra one being due to the addition of the Winter Games.

The I.O.C. is the absolute supreme authority as far as the Games are concerned, but the National Olympic Committees have an important role, for they are responsible for nominating the Olympic teams. The International Sports Federations have an equally important role to play, but they must come under the approval of the I.O.C. Only one international Sport Federation is recognized for each sport, there being at the moment twenty-six.

The headquarters of the I.O.C. are, at the moment, situated in Lausanne, Switzerland.

Article 30 of the I.O.C. Regulations states that at least fifteen of the sports listed must be included in the official program of any of the Games. All the events of the program must be completed within fifteen days, or within ten days for the Winter Games. It will be noted that in the list given below athletics counts as only one; the list is alphabetical but based on French terminology:

athletics (track and field)
rowing
basketball
boxing
canoeing
cycling
fencing
football
gymnastics
weight lifting
handball
hockey
judo
wrestling
swimming and diving
modern pentathlon

equestrian sports
shooting
archery
volleyball
water polo
yachting

Of these the equestrian sports are held on the last day because of the technical reason that the horses are likely to leave their marks on the arena.

FINE ARTS

The Olympic Games may also, or rather should also, include a manifestation of the fine arts, including architecture, literature, music, painting, sculpture, and even sports philately and photography. Olympic Medals in these categories have been given at the Games from Stockholm in 1912 until London in 1948, especially for the first five of the above list. Sometimes there were more and sometimes fewer sections of the fine arts competitions, which all had to be connected with a sports theme.

The gods of antiquity had given their blessings to the exhibition of works of art just as they had done to the victorious athletes. Pierre de Coubertin was most anxious that the modern Games should include cultural manifestations other than the athletic. This principle also has the most firm support of Mr. Avery Brundage. Coubertin himself entered an essay, under a pseudonym, and it was not till years afterward that it became known that he was the gold-medalist winner.

At present the host city makes a point of organizing exhibitions of national popular art. Part of the purpose of the Games is that the peoples should get to know each other, and art is palpably one of the best media for this purpose. The Mexico City Games extended these manifestations in not confining them to the popular and other arts of their own country, inviting many displays from other nations.

There have been difficulties, and in particular there was the question of judging, especially with the different languages, but this can certainly be overcome as it has been earlier, and following the example of the annual Nobel prize, which has surmounted this obstacle completely. A question that had been raised on an occasion was the fact that artists are necessarily professionals and not amateurs, but this should not be a serious difficulty.

Such manifestations contribute to the formation of the fully integrated man, not only with the physical but in other cultural aspects. The present tendency is to include art in the Olympic Games, but not as competitions, as had been previously tried. In all probability the main reason why the art competitions failed was that they would require a set of officials different from those preoccupied with the Games, and the Games themselves now require such immense organization, including major constructional works, that the work has to be taken in hand well before the previous Olympiad.

The role of art in the ancient Games has been referred to by the late Carl Diem in a 1962 Academy lecture:

"Not only did visitors have before their eyes the sacred spring of life in the throng of competitors, an impression which anyone may feel who experiences the Olympic Games today, but they also heard the intellectual elite of their people and saw them face-to-face at the lectures for which people foregathered in the Altis. These lectures were delivered from the top of the steps of the Opisthodromos to the surrounding crowd. We know what great men showed themselves there, such as Miltiades, the victor of Marathon, whose helmet was found in the course of our excavations; Themistocles, the victor of Salamis; philosophers and artists of all ages, from Cheiron and Thales (who both died at Olympia) to Plato; poets such as Simonides and Euripides; artists such as Phidias and Aethion; and writers such as Lucian, who claimed to have been there eight times. Similar lectures were also held at Elis in the period of preparation. Herodotos read the nine books of his history from the Temple of Zeus, and it was here that Thucydides conceived the idea of his research into the causes and effects of the Peloponnesian War. . . . In the year A.D. 97 [219th Olympiad] the cynic philosopher Dion Chrysostomos delivered from this same pulpit his twelfth Olympic address, consisting of the most comprehensive statement of the meaning of the Olympic Games."

This is only one of the verbal pictures that the late Carl Diem has so skillfully portrayed for us. It makes it clear why Mr. Avery Brundage should insist that the fine arts were essentially part of the ancient Olympic Games and why he was so keen that they should once more be more closely associated with the contemporary Games.

The Olympic Games make us realize that the I.O.C. is primarily concerned with athletics, but its jurisdiction and concern are in reality far greater. It is an orchestrator of all forms of sport. It has many matters on its plate and some are not so urgent as others, and that is probably why the I.O.C. has not acted even more energetically on the question of art exhibits or competitions. Other matters, such as the participation of women in sports, are matters that tend to settle themselves and that are most definitely beyond its scope but that require guided evolution rather than chirurgical intervention. The urgent matters, the big headaches, are not the matters of broad general principles, but the susceptibilites of individual nations, or even more so the susceptibilities of nations against neighbors, unfortunately sometimes in a political aspect.

We have already dealt with the headache of amateur status. It is in a state of eruption, but hardly an explosive eruption, and is being kept within confines. Conditions of life are so much outside the control of the individual, and are continually rapidly evolving. The present tendency is more to examine the whole question on a broader plane. The tendency, but let us insist that it is as yet only a tendency, is to examine whether the competitor has a main trade or profession assuring him his livelihood, whether he is neglecting his trade or even more so his studies for the sake of participation, and whether he is participating with the object of acquiring material advantage, permanently or otherwise. The I.O.C., however, is still very conscious that if it gives in an inch in the amateur status regulations there will be competitors who will immediately try to stretch it to a mile.

The objects and consequent problems of the I.O.C. were expressed exceptionally clearly, even if not directly, by its President, Avery Brundage, in an address delivered at the Sorbonne in June, 1964:

"One does not yet generally understand that the revival of the Olympic Games constituted only the first phase of the programme of Coubertin. The Games were to stimulate the governments, educators and the public, the desire to create national programmes of physical education and of amateur competitive sport, which would assist in the following tasks: eradicate social injustice, to combat the increasing materialism of our epoch, correct the effects of industrialization and urbanization in the extreme, which destroy both health and morality. Further, through the extension of the ancient Greek idea, then nationalistic, they should create and develop friendship and goodwill."

VIII
WOMEN AND
THE OLYMPIC GAMES

The attitude of the sports and games authorities as to the propriety of women in sports would appear to be very much as it should be. Let the women settle the whole question of participation themselves. Whereas the amateur status question is a matter of ceaseless discussion, the question of women in sports, which is also a question equally in evolution, is taking a smooth course. There is, however, a most important question as regards women, namely that nowadays the possibilities of physical education and also of practicing sports and athletics is very much one of the grounds, appliances and equipment being made available. These especially in schools are usually supplied by the government, and on this point, in most countries, women have a very real cause for complaint.

Coubertin was in principle against the participation of women in the Olympic Games. He indicated that their role should be confined to crowning the victors with garlands. This does not mean that Coubertin was against women in sports in general. We might reflect that at the time when Coubertin was proposing the revival of the Games the world was quite different in outlook and life than it is now. It was a time when the paterfamilias ruled supremely over his subject family and used threats of hell fires of the world to come in order to intimidate it.

It would surely be a misconception to expect that women should, or could be able to do everything that men do in sports, though it is worth noting that in the original Games of 1896 competitors could take part "without racial or sex discrimination."

It is proper that men should be fast of foot and strong. It is proper that women should be graceful. There are of course many men who are not made that way and try to be graceful, and most people anything but approve of such feminine manners for men. Why should we not therefore disapprove of women with masculine manners? Fortunately we realize that the participation of women in sport in general is nothing of the sort but it is not everyone who is assured that it is not injurious to their health. It is an idea that is not dying out quite as quickly as it should.

The atitude of the I.O.C. and of sports authorities in general is therefore sound. Let the whole thing settle itself. We have, however, just indicated the just complaint that too large a proportion of public funds goes to the supplying of opportunities to men only.

The Soviet authorities were generally more advanced than other countries in the question of tending to the women's demand for athletic opportunities, and even to the supply of these before the actual demand though we must comment that this was largely for gymnastics and athletics and not for that element of sport understood by play, games, and fun. Some years ago we did see some beefy women Olympic champions, but their participation did not meet with public approval, either by men or women, and this would seem to have readjusted itself, among athletic women competitors.

The question of the propriety of women's participation in sports is that of the extent to which communities, of both men and women, think of it in each particular land, and of how much the women are influenced by this public opinion. There can be no doubt but that women conform to a considerable extent to the type that their menfolk wish them to be. And why not? For do not men, even if in a more unobtrusive way, behave in a way which they think would be attractive to women—even if they are not willing to admit it?

There is another aspect too. Women do not so easily participate in team games for women only. Hockey? Yes. Ice hockey? No. Football? No. Rugby? Definitely no. Basketball? Certainly.

Why not? Perhaps because some of these sports are not suitable. Nonparticipation in some team games by women may also be due to two factors: the one being their character, but the other their mode of life. All big cities have hundreds of men's clubs, with perhaps sometimes a ladies' annex. Women's clubs very soon obtain a mixed character or close down. Is it a question of women's character? Partly, possibly, but men's work finishes with the close of office hours, while women's work is never done. Yes, but it is more than this; choose your own explanation. In any case women are not prone to forming women's clubs, including those that might promote team games.

All this may change and rapidly. At the time of the outbreak of World War I, a woman at the wheel of a car was a comparative rarity, looked upon by some men with admiration and by some with strong disapproval. The question of women in athletics, as distinct from sports in general, is settling itself, but it still has many aspects of controversial discussion.

In the Summer Session of the International Olympic Academy of 1964, the question of women's participation in athletics and sport was the subject of three lectures. In the past generation an objection to women's participation was on the question of possible injury to their health. Professor Liselott Diem contended that women athletes have easier childbirth. Dr. Henri Pouret, a gynecologist, said that this was not his experience. Here were two opinions in opposition. It is possible to argue that sport might result in easier childbirth for the normal woman, but it is precisely the women who have strong muscles, and who might thus expect difficult childbirth, who indulge in sports. Our sole comment is that this is a subject beyond our ken; we hope that others will investigate it more thoroughly for us. It has been known that in backward rural countries a woman might go to the fields, holding a toddler by the hand, and return with two children. In the meantime, fortunately, the question of sport being injurious to women's health in general is a bugbear of the past. Only fifty years ago it was considered injurious for women to ride other than sidesaddle.

Quite another question is as to whether the bearing of children is detrimental to the achievement of fine performances by women in athletics. Here Mrs. Diem assures us that it is quite the contrary and that women obtain better achievements after childbirth. She quotes authorities to support her statement and reminds us that Fanny Blankers-Koen, the outstanding athlete of the 1948 London Games, known as the Flying Dutchwoman, was then the mother of two children and yet managed to collect four gold medals.

At the 1964 summer session, Dr. Eva Földes, the Hungarian authoress, reviewed the history of women in sport throughout the ages. In Egyptian and especially in the ancient Cretan times, she tells us, the women indulged in all forms of sports, including that of somersaulting over the backs of gigantic bulls, of which Cretan frescoes still survive to prove it.

We can go back to the ancient Greeks for guidance on the question of women in sports, just as we can for so many other aspects of life and culture. The very early history of the Olympic Games, to which we did not refer in earlier chapters, indicates that the earliest races were for women. To quote Dr. Földes:

"Hippodamia organized a bodyguard of sixteen virgins who had to weave a veil for the goddess Hera every four years, and then in honor of the goddess a race was performed in Olympia. Thus Hippodamia established the Hera Games. Every four years the race took place in the dales of Olympia and the festivities were mainly religious. The race was a single item. The virgins were grouped into three age groups and, as Pausanias writes, they raced over a distance that corresponds to 160.22 meters. The winners received laurel wreaths and a part of the cow that was sacrificed to Hera. The participants, to judge from the existing statues, ran with flowing hair; their skirts were above the knees and their right breasts exposed. (Queen Victoria would not have been amused!) We may note that the Greeks of those times had already developed the idea of handicaps, as shown by the age groups."

The seclusion of women in Western Europe and their consequent restriction from many sports was Victorian. It was an era in which the propriety pendulum had swung back too far.

Dr. Eleanor Metheny, President of the American Academy of Physical Education, speaking at the 1964 summer session, referred to ancient Greek mythology to demonstrate the attitude toward women in sports. It would seem not to have been very different from present popular conception and may be educative for us.

"The image projected by the female gods," she said, "is almost totally devoid of any suggestion of physical prowess. Skill, rather than strength, is assigned to the huntress Artemis; and while the intellectual powers of Athena were unsurpassed, the spear she carried was a symbol of her authority rather than an actual weapon. But it appears that female skill had to be paid for by denial of normal sexual powers. The cult of Artemis rejected men; and the eternal virginity of Athena is consecrated in the temple called the Parthenon."

"In Demeter" she goes on to say, "the primary female role is epitomized in the concept of the Earth Mother, as the ground in which life is bred and nurtured. Hera, the godly representative of the wife, is pictured as a helpmate. . . . The image of Aphrodite is in sharp contrast with the image of these homely female virtues. She is pictured as the Goddess of Beauty, infinitely desirable by all men. . . . But a more comprehensive image is projected by Hippolyta, the kinglike queen of the Amazons, who won the enduring love of Theseus. . . . To Theseus, Hippolyta represented everything a man might hope to find in a woman, but it must be recorded that she was rejected by the men and women of Athens."

We are very thankful to Dr. Metheny for this picture, of which we have given but a very small extract. It reveals the wisdom of the ancient Greeks, who realized that there was not only one type of woman to consider. We would be foolish if we attempted to conjure up the ideal of the sportswoman and sought to indicate what her nature should be. Attitudes can change so rapidly too. Think of the differences in the tasks that the women of wartorn Europe were called on to perform in behalf of their countries in World War II as compared with World War I. At the turn of the present century women were unhealthily dressed in tight whalebone corseted cages with bustles that in no circumstances would allow of athletic movement. If women so much as showed an ankle below their floor-sweeping skirts, such brazen immorality would have damned their reputations for ever.

Now let us glance at the history of women in the Olympic Games of the modern era. In the 1896 Games in Athens no women took part, in spite of the ambitions of a fair Athenian. Dr. Földes has described the occasion as follows:

"In 1896 in Athens there was a pioneer lady, Melpomene, who trained secretly for three weeks, and presented her nomination in the modern Olympics for participation in the Marathon race. Her request was refused, but she was determined. Accompanied by some of her acquaintances on bicycles she set out from Marathon to Athens and allegedly covered the distance of forty-two kilometres in four and a half hours."

The Greek paper *Acropolis* did not disregard this spectacular event. It wrote: "The Olympic Committee deserved to be reprimanded, because it was discourteous in refusing a lady's nomination. We can assure those concerned that none of the participants would have had any objections."

We agree, but it would have been a case of a lady running after the men. We might note, nonetheless, that in matters of endurance women come far closer to men than in matters of speed.

The participation of women in the Olympic Games was very gradual and did not obtain ready approval.

In 1900, in Paris, women participated for the first time, but only in tennis.

In 1904, in St. Louis, archery was added.

In 1908, in London, figure skating was added, but it did not form part of the official Games.

In 1912, in Stockholm, swimming figured for women.

In 1924, in Paris, there was a woman's event for fencing, and women participated in the Chamonix Winter Games.

Then, in 1926, at a meeting of the I.O.C., on a proposal of Mr. Edstrom, the I.O.C. approved the admittance of women to a limited number of competitions during the Olympic Games. Three months later the International Track and Field Association of Amateurs confirmed this, but women were to be taken into the Olympic Games "on trial." As a result, women took part in athletics in the Amsterdam Olympic Games of 1928, for the first time.

It was not really till after World War II at the London Olympic Games that women took part in the Games in anything like the proportions of the subsequent Rome and Tokyo Games.

And so, what is our conclusion? The benefit of sport in the formation of character and the development of fully integrated persons, sound in mind and body, cannot be the prerogative of men only. Let us also not forget the dictum of Pierre de Coubertin: "If one hundred young people [and he did not say men] train their bodies twenty must specialize, and if twenty do this, five become models due to their excellent performance."

This applies, of course, equally as strongly to women as to men as regards the highest level sports and athletics. Their participation is of far greater importance to the well-being of women in general than to the small number of competitors who enter with the ambition of becoming champions.

Let us remember that the ancient Greeks entrusted the complete upbringing of their children up to the age of seven to their womenfolk, for on them the future of the race depended. Is it not then of importance that the women should also be brought up to become fully integrated? Even if we somewhat disregard sports for grown women, we should at least see to it that proper provision is made for schoolgirls, and remember that sport is no longer to be considered a luxury but an essential part of education and upbringing.

There are some very attractive women in sports and in the Olympic Games, and since there is no longer any question about sports being detrimental to their health, that should be as complete an answer to any who wish to oppose them—and besides there can be few things more attractive and more beautiful than a woman skater or diver.

IX
IDEOLOGY
AND PROBLEMS

We have now examined cursorily the ingredients that constitute the Olympic Games, their history generally, and the purposes that prompted their revival.

We can now examine more closely the promotion of the ideology of the Games, the purpose of what is called the Olympic Movement, and the problems that beset it.

The problems have arisen because, as Mr. Brundage put it, "The success of the Games has been far too rapid and the evils have tended to get beyond the control of the handful of amateurs whose care it is to guide the evolution of sport, especially through the resplendent model of the Games."

The sixty-eight years that have elapsed from Athens to Tokyo, or the seventy-two to Mexico City, comprise only sixteen actual Games (since three were canceled for the war years). At a maximum of two weeks each, that gives a total of only thirty-two weeks of actual Games, plus the odd twelve weeks for the Winter Games.

Mr. Brundage, speaking in Athens on June 16, 1961, stated: "We have many problems due to the astonishingly rapid growth of the Games, since there has not been time without organization of volunteers to educate everyone in Olympic principles. The International Olympic Committee was placed in charge of the Olympic Movement, with the duty to maintain its ideals and defend its principles. We must restate and clearly define our objectives and draft our rules accordingly. . . . The objective of the Olympic Movement as designed by the Baron Pierre de Coubertin, is a broad and comprehensive development for men, in which sport, emphasizing grace, beauty and the moral qualities, plays a part, but only a part. Athletic games and competitions are not a career—they are incidental of symmetrical and harmonious physical, mental and spiritual development, a supplement and not a goal."

This concise statement by the President of the I.O.C. is probably the most elucidating yet made on the whole question of the ideology and problems of the Olympics.

The Olympic Games have seized the imagination of the public at large, but Coubertin's purpose was to get to the core of the problem, to utilize the Games to influence the responsible Governmental authorities to act. They have indeed reacted but we may well wonder whether some have reacted too fast, and others too slowly. Whatever the situation in each country attitudes in general have not developed along similar lines, with the result that governmental encouragement and conditions of training in each country are no longer entirely similar.

In 1963 Mr. Brundage said:

"The Olympic Games were not revived by the Baron Pierre de Coubertin merely to give contestants a chance to win medals and to break records, not to entertain the public, not to provide for the participants a stepping-stone to a career in professional sport, and certainly not to demonstrate the superiority of one political system over another.

"His idea was that they would:

"1. bring to the attention of the world the fact that a national program of physical training and competitive sport will not only develop stronger and healthier boys and girls but also, and perhaps more important, will make better citizens through the character-building that follows participation in properly administered amateur sport;

"2. demonstrate the principles of fair play and good sportsmanship, which could be adopted with greater advantage in any other spheres of activity;

"3. stimulate interest in the fine arts through exhibitions and demonstrations, and thus contribute to a broader and more well-rounded life;

"4. teach that sport is play for fun and enjoyment and not to make money, and that with devotion to the task in hand the reward will take care of itself; the philosophy of amateurism as contrasted to that of materialism;

"5. create international amity and good will, thus leading to a happier and more peaceful world."

It would be going too far to say that improprieties occur in any countries. We are not too happy with what we call state aid in some countries, but this is very largely due, perhaps entirely due, to a historic background whereby private enterprise has never had a chance to take the initiative. We are afraid that this may result in unfair assistance to athletes in international contests. It would be nonetheless even more disappointing if such nations neglected to pay attention to the inclusion of physical education in their school curricula.

All present-day writers on sports insist, and do so categorically, that the basis of sports should be the element of "play" and that the element of compulsion can be detrimental in the extreme. Sport and play for the fun of it must be the outstanding reason for indulging in them.

Peter C. McIntosh, chief physical education officer for Greater London, has some pithy remarks to offer in this regard. He indicates that physical education should be a question of "fitness for sport" rather than "sport for fitness." "If a game is worth playing," he says, "then it is worth playing badly." By this he means that games are to be played to be enjoyed and should not be restricted to those who excel in them.

Many golfers, for instance, lose most of the fun when they become proficient. The mediocre player will return to the clubhouse after his round mentally wagging his tail because of some half dozen strokes that he played above his average ability at some of the holes, and especially happy that he put up a good game against his opponent, whether he won or lost. The expert golfer is likely to return to the clubhouse in an irritable mood because his round included three or four strokes that were not of his best.

The motto that Coubertin adopted and promoted was written

in enormous letters over the Wembley Stadium for the 1948 Games. It was first propounded by a Bishop of Pennsylvania, though it is generally ascribed erroneously to Coubertin himself: "The most important thing in the Olympic Games is not to win but to take part, as the most important thing in life is not the triumph but the struggle. The essential is not to have conquered but to have fought well."

This very motto is at the heart of the total prohibition of professionals in the Games. The important thing for a professional is to win, not just to take part. It is of course quite impossible to exercise control over the spirit of the competitors; thus, in spite of the fact that there are many professionals who compete with the true spirit of the amateur (as there are also amateurs, or rather pseudo-amateurs, who compete with the outlook of a professional), we have to create regulations that define who is an amateur and who is not.

The I.O.C. booklet of 1962, Part IV, Rule 26, defines the amateur as follows:

"An amateur is one who participates and always has participated in sport as an avocation without any material gain of any kind.

"He does not qualify:

"a) if he has not a basic occupation designed to insure his present and future livelihood;

"b) if he receives or has received remuneration for participation in sport;

"c) if he does not comply with the Rules of the International Federation concerned and the official interpretation of this Rule, No. 26."

The intention of this rule is quite clear, but the interpretation is not always too easy. Athletes who participate in the Olympic Games are financed by their national Olympic committee. Their journey to and from the city of the Games is paid; their board and lodging and also a reasonable amount of pocket money are given. Well and good, but what happens if this is done for Games other than the Olympic, and regularly? The facts are generally sufficient for a correct judgment, but some National Olympic Committees take a broader, or narrower, view than others and a doubtful amateur might scrape through in one country when he would not have done so in another. What happens when the state gives assistance by securing a job for a champion which he would not have got if he had not been such a champion with a likelihood of bringing glory to his national colors, now or later?

Some aspects are unavoidably hard or harsh. If a coach or trainer works for profit he is barred from participating as an amateur, and yet he is an educator with a profession designed to secure his present and future livelihood. He is, of course, interested professionally in the success of the competitors under his care and tuition. The doctor who cares and tends for the same athlete, and advises him on his diet and health, professionally, is nonetheless not debarred.

What about the young athlete who receives great privileges from his firm, time off, holidays with pay and the like, which he would not have received if he were not a budding champion likely to reap glory for his firm? He will be reckoned as no longer qualifying as an amateur, but if his father were wealthy enough to pay for that very same holiday, what then? We can rest assured that the Members of the I.O.C., individually and as a whole, are absolutely aware of all the difficulties and resolve them in the best possible way, ready to readjust with changing conditions.

Mr. Otto Szymiczek, the Curator of the International Olympic Academy, covered all these contingencies when he said: "The regulations foresee up to what point the privileges may reach, but it is not possible for them to cover the motivations of the privileges, their derivation and the objectives intended by their being granted." The President of the I.O.C. had the following comments to make on the subject:

"Every competitor in the Olympic Games must sign an entry form, testifying that he is an amateur, according to the regulations, and this must be certified by his National Federation and by his National Olympic Committee. If any nonamateur has participated in the Olympic Games, at least three people have lied." He has also pointed out that the Olympic Games depend upon a world movement of hundreds of millions of amateurs by comparison with whom the professionals are numerically negligible.

The Olympic Movement is faced with ills and dangers, but what institution is not? Pseudo-amateurism is one, but probably not so great since all sport authorities are alerted to it. The commercial exploitation of sport by the "managers" is another, and probably far worse. The greatest is the ignorance as to the significance of sport by the public at large and especially of the ideology by youth in its formative age. Governments, too, can be an even greater menace.

Let us particularly note that the contemporary Olympic Movement has succeeded in obtaining the acknowledgment of all religions. A tangible proof of this is the pronouncement on April 28, 1966, by Pontifex Paul VI, Pope of Rome, on the occasion of the audience of the Members of the International Olympic Committee at the Vatican.

During this pronouncement the Pontifex asked himself what possible relationship there might be between sports, on the one hand, which deal with body and muscles of man, and religion, on the other hand, which turns the soul and spirit of man toward God. Sports teach struggle, endeavor, and victory over the opponent, whereas religion teaches concord, harmony, brotherhood, suppression of antagonism, and social peace. And he himself gives the reply:

"Whether she [the Church] considers sport as a physical education, as moral and social education, or as international education, in all three of these fields she discovers not only certain points in common, but certain profound harmonies and, as it were, certain relationships between the healthy practice of sport and her own doctrine. Is this really so surprising? Is it not the same God who created man's soul and his body? moral beauty and physical beauty? Let us not fear then: the true God is the friend of life, which He created, and cannot but approve competition and sport, provided these are based on mutual respect and on the desire for man's true well-being."

Both religion and sports, then, have the same objective, the perfection of man, who is the creature of God. This too was the belief of the priests of yore in the sacred Altis of Olympia.

X

THE INTERNATIONAL OLYMPIC ACADEMY

In the previous pages mention has been made several times of the International Olympic Academy. It was founded to propagate the knowledge of the Olympic ideology to all interested in sport, and to be in the nature of a research workshop.

In 1927 the late John Ketseas, a member of the I.O.C. for Greece, who died early in 1965, conceived the idea of establishing such an institute in Greece, to attend to such matters, and a law was then passed to establish it. Unfortunately, the director of physical education of the country, John Chrysaphis, a truly outstanding sports ideologist and practical man, died suddenly, with the result that the idea was shelved.

Much water ran through the Alpheus before the idea was again actively pursued. Let us quote from Otto Szymiczek, the Curator of the Academy, at the 1964 Session:

"In his explanatory note, which he submitted in 1949 to the I.O.C., Mr. John Ketseas, permanent representative of the I.O.C. to Greece, refers to the following:

"'Already in 1927, the Baron de Coubertin, while in Athens, expressed to me his fears that the mechanization and training to the hilt of the athletes would be an outcome detrimental to the necessary equipoise between the body and the mind.'"

"The Olympic Games," Coubertin had stressed, "must be enriched with history, art and philosophy; they must establish noble traditions, impart rhythm and beauty, and preserve with zeal a moderate and proper proportion in all things, and organize themselves with a continuous and creative course in view, far from passions, passing caprices, and hesitations."

"One can thus say," Mr. Szymiczek stated, "that the planting of the seed of a special spiritual center, of an organ that would undertake the work of the dissemination of the Olympic ideology and the correct teaching of the Olympic spirit, existed in the thoughts and intentions of the Baron Pierre de Coubertin, who, in a letter of March 16, 1937, to the German government, becomes decisive and clear when he proposes the establishment of the International Olympic Institute, as a center of Olympic studies, to which would be entrusted the study of the documents of his archives relative to the revival of the contemporary Olympic Games. Coubertin's proposal was accepted and a sum was set aside from the income of the Olympic Games of 1936 (Berlin) for the issue of the *Olympic Review* (1938-1944) in the form of a three-language official periodical of the Olympic movement.

"During 1938 the elaboration of a plan was evolved by Carl Diem and John Ketseas for the establishment of an international center of research with the object of the study of Olympic matters that would function in the genuine environment of the Olympic Games, that is in ancient Olympia. On June 19, 1947, during the session of the I.O.C. at Stockholm, Mr. Ketseas officially introduced the thought of the foundation of a research center, and the President of the I.O.C., Mr. Avery Brundage, realizing the importance of the proposal, expressed himself most favorably for it. In January 1949 Mr. Ketseas presented an explanatory report regarding the planned establishment of an Olympic Academy in Greece. In the compilation of the memorandum he had worked very closely with the late Carl Diem. Finally came the historic date upon which the foundation of the International Olympic Academy was approved—April 28, 1949, when, during a session of the I.O.C. in Rome, after an introduction by John Ketseas, the establishment was decided upon, with headquarters at Olympia.

"The Hellenic Olympic Committee, which undertook this honorable assignment, immediately sent invitations for the realization of the first session. Unfortunately, however, from the totality of the Olympic Committees of that year, then numbering eighty, only four replied, and they in the negative."

Ketseas and Diem were not to be put off, but the waters of the Alpheus had to run for a further twelve years, until the occasion of the meeting of the I.O.C. in Athens in 1961.

The German Archaeological Society had just completed the excavations of the ancient stadion at Olympia, for which it had the concession of the Greek Archaeological Society, and was then due to hand it over to the latter. It was decided to take advantage of this occasion and hold the first Session of the Academy in June. The sum for the excavations of the ancient stadion was provided as a seventy-fifth birthday present to Carl Diem by the German Olympic Committee, through the initiative of its President, Mr. Willi Daume. Mr. Daume also promised, for the same occasion, that "as far as the German side could contribute to it, we would help to create the Academy."

The German Olympic Committee stood by its word, and the Hellenic Olympic Committee gave its equal support. Carl Diem, as head of the Cologne High School of Sport, brought a team of students from Germany, while Mr. Cleanthis Palaeologos, his counterpart from Athens, did likewise. Lecturers of world repute were invited, and students of many countries took part. For this Session there were gymnastic displays, which have since been discontinued.

Subsequently the Hellenic Olympic Committee took the Academy more firmly under its wing and at a considerable expense bought the whole of the property bordering the ancient stadion to the north and on the eastern foothills of the Cronion Hill, now some hundred and fifty acres in all. Plans were drawn up for the erection of the requisite buildings, ultimately to house four or five hundred students and lecturers of both sexes, together with the requisite refectories, gymnasia, library, and a building to house the Academy's museum of the Contemporary Olympic Games.

The erection of the buildings has necessarily been somewhat slow, but since 1967 well over a hundred participants have been domiciled in the new installations. One of the first tasks of the Academy, it was deemed proper, should be the hollowing out of a large basin in the property, the Coubertin Grove, whereby a drive bordered by cyperissus trees leads to the commemorative stele in which the heart of the reviver of the Games resposes eternally. This has been carried out in such a manner that the Academy itself can be considered as the prime memorial to the great Frenchman.

To participate in the Sessions of the Academy the students have to be nominated or approved by their National Olympic Committees, though this is really a typical requirement just to insure that the students should be of the necessary educational level. It is intended, and hoped, that with the completion of the buildings, or even before, there will be sessions at many periods of the year, for specialized groups, such as sports authors, pressmen, and sports medical experts, physical education teachers, and possibly even for champion athletes.

The lectures cover all aspects of the Olympic Movement: ideology, history of the ancient and modern Games, psychology, scientific and medical matters, and techniques connected with sports. Importance is attached to seminars and discussions.

And now let us consider the present Olympic outlook and its projection into the future. Let us listen once more to Mr. Otto Szymiczek speaking in the 1964 session:

"The year 1964 constitutes a significant milestone in the history of the contemporary Olympic Games. The Winter Games at Innsbruck, Austria, as also the athletic Olympiad of Tokyo, Japan, were so successful from the organizational aspect, by the participation of athletes and the presence of philathletes, that one might express the opinion that perfection has been achieved. The carrying out of the contests in every sphere of sport was admirable. The achievement of the athletes surpassed every previous standard, and hundreds of thousands of spectators enjoyed a high level of competition in the various sports. With the help of contemporary technical methods hundreds of millions of people were able to follow the superlative competitions.

"Twice the Gold Medalist King of the Hellenes (Innsbruck and Tokyo) handed over the Olympic Flame from the Sacred Altis, proclaiming the high ideals of the Games. The Olympic

Flame shone for the first time in Asia, where millions of people welcomed it with emotion and demonstrated their deep faith in the Olympic Spirit and in the value of the Games.

"As I now recollect this recent and replete past, and concentrating my fulsome impressions, I can categorically assert that the Olympic Movement finds itself upon the best path for the fulfilment of its great and high ideals."

Mr. Szymiczek went on to say that he had no fault to find with the organizers, the paid personnel, the umpires and judges, the leaders and those who accompanied the teams, or the coaches. The contestants, he said, "proved themselves to be worthy of the Olympic participation and took part honestly, maintaining the rules of the Games. . . . A noble and knightly spirit reigned among those who took part and in the true Olympic Spirit, friendships were created regardless of political, religious, racial or other distinctions."

Since the Session of 1966 H.R.H. George W. Prince of Hanover, LL.D., has been President of the Academy, and follows the slightest detail of its functioning, presiding at all lectures, seminars, and discussions. The I.O.C. has also appointed a commission, with Mr. Ivar Vind of Denmark as its President, which collaborates closely with the Executive Committee of the Academy, and whose members also attend the sessions.

There are difficulties, problems, material outlooks, which the Olympic Movement has to face, but there are also aspects of progress, of internationalism and of amity and of so much expression of true sportsmanship that our hopes can remain high that the role of sport in the culture and civilization of mankind is gradually coming into its own.

INDEX

Words used throughout the book have been omitted, such as athlete, athletic, contest, competitor, Greece, Greek, Olympic Games, Olympia.

99